SMOKE AND MIRRORS

'This is a simply splendid book. Jim Brown argues with vigour and wit for a strongly positive view of scientific realism. He puts his own arguments fairly and openly, showing that no one should lightly dismiss his case. In a comprehensive review, which itself justifies the work, he presents the positions of those whom he would refute with clarity and sympathy. Taking on a multitude of recent advocates of scientific anti-realism, he shows their weaknesses with a scalpel-like critical faculty. As one who is at the receiving end of Brown's attack, I very much hope that he is wrong. I fear he may be right.'

Michael Ruse, *University of Guelph*

Realism is an enlightening story and wholly believable; yet this wonderful picture of humanity's best efforts at knowledge has been badly bruised. *Smoke and Mirrors* fights back. But this volume is not wholly devoted to combating Rorty and others who blow smoke in our eyes; the second half is concerned with arguing that there are some amazing ways in which science mirrors the world; *abstraction, abstract objects*, and *a priori* ways of getting at reality are the particular focus of interest.

James Robert Brown is Professor of Philosophy at the University of Toronto. His research interests include the philosophy of mathematics, foundations of physics, social relations of science, and thought experiments, as well as more general issues in the philosophy of science. He is the author of two earlier books: *The Rational and the Social* and *The Laboratory of the Mind* which are both available from Routledge.

PHILOSOPHICAL ISSUES IN SCIENCE SERIES
Edited by W.H. Newton-Smith

SMOKE AND MIRRORS

How science reflects reality

James Robert Brown

London and New York

First published 1994
by Routledge
11 Fetter Lane, London EC4P 4EE

Simultaneously published in the USA and Canada
by Routledge
29 West 35th Street, New York, NY 10001

© 1994 James Robert Brown

Set in 10/12 pt Palatino by
Florencetype Ltd, Kewstoke, Avon
Printed and bound in Great Britain by
T J Press Ltd, Padstow, Cornwall

British Library Cataloguing in Publication Data
A catalogue record for this book is available from the British Library

Library of Congress Cataloging in Publication Data
Brown, James Robert.
Smoke and mirrors : how science reflects reality / James Robert Brown.
p.   cm. – (Philosophical issues in science)
Includes bibliographical references and index.
1. Realism. 2. Science – Philosophy. I. Title. II. Series.
B835.B86 1993
149′.2–dc20   93–25307
CIP

ISBN 0–415–09180–2   0–415–09181–0 (pbk)

To Lars, Sławek, Srđan,
Elena, Jürgen, Bill and Kathy,
and especially to
Dubrovnik

CONTENTS

CONTENTS

PREFACE

If I were Bertrand Russell (who I'm not) and this book sold for a shilling (which it doesn't), then I'd call it a 'shilling shocker', since it's sure to annoy many readers. The title alludes to those like Rorty who dismiss the attempts of science to mirror reality. But it also pokes a bit of fun at my own very platonistic views of how that mirroring of nature works. The first chapter may seem harmless; it is a defence of realism – though rather unusual – and it provides a mind-set, an outlook, for all that follows. After the stage is set with the first chapter, the next four (in Part II: Smoke) are largely negative. These four chapters attack relativists, naturalists, verificationists and anthropologists-in-the-lab, each and every one of them in their various ways an enemy of science (i.e. they don't share my somewhat romanticized view). But even those who might be tempted to cheer me on in these early chapters will probably be unpleasantly surprised at the more positive views spelled out in the later parts of the book (in Part III: Mirrors). The homage paid in the last four chapters to abstract entities and to the a priori way science reflects reality is sure to arouse widespread disapproval. But, if none of this is convincing, I hope people at least find it all a good read. I'm well aware, though, that I've not sufficiently heeded the advice of Jean Cocteau: 'Mirrors should reflect a little before throwing back images.'

ACKNOWLEDGEMENTS

I wish to thank Andrew Irvine, William Newton-Smith, Kathleen Okruhlik, Mary Tiles, and especially Randall Keen who provided me with an extraordinary amount of very useful commentary and also prepared the index. I am also grateful to David Kotchan (once again) for many of the diagrams. Finally I wish to acknowledge with thanks the very generous help of S.S.H.R.C.

Part I

INTRODUCTION

The first chapter is a defence of realism. It employs a kind of 'realism is the best explanation of the success of science' argument, but it is quite different from other versions in that the explanation is *narrative* – a style of explanation often used in biology and in history. The conclusion of the argument – full-blooded scientific and metaphysical realism – is strong, though the argument for it is not. (Of course, it would be better to have a strong argument for a weak conclusion, but why not take a chance?) Normally, 'success of science' arguments model the explanation on deductive or inductive forms. Critics then ask embarrassing questions about novel predictions and the like, knowing full well there are no answers to be had. Instead, I see realism as an enlightening story, a tale which enriches our experience and makes it more intelligible. But it is not just another tall tale; I'm not embracing anti-realism at some meta-level. Instead, just as biological and historical accounts of past events explain by telling a story in which the explained events are embedded, realism provides a general framework for understanding how things work. For that reason, it is quite believable and should be thought true.

1

EXPLAINING THE SUCCESS OF SCIENCE

Richard Rorty's *Philosophy and the Mirror of Nature* (1979) has done much to undermine a particular view of scientific knowledge and intellectual progress. More recently, he has pooh-poohed the very idea of 'explaining the success of science', and with it he has dismissed one of the stronger arguments for scientific realism. (The argument runs: our theories are successful and truth is the best explanation for this success; therefore, our theories are probably true.) '[W]e do not itch,' says Rorty, 'for an explanation of the success of recent Western science any more than for the success of recent Western politics' (1987, 41). Written just before the collapse of the Berlin Wall, the dissolution of the Warsaw Pact, the break-up of the Soviet Union and the crushing of Iraq in the Gulf War, it is hard to imagine a less plausible sentiment.

Not only are we at present swamped with (usually silly and smug) analyses of 'why the West won', but if events should turn sour (as they often seem in danger of doing) we will be awash with explanations of the 'failure' of Western policies. And our concern is quite fitting. Knowing why particular political strategies worked (or failed) is of obvious vital interest. The same can be said for science. I'm happy to join Rorty in lumping science and politics together, but let's try to explain the successes (or failures) of both, rather than turn our backs on them.

Karl Popper has a completely different motivation, but he too has steadfastly held that the success of science is not to be explained – it's a miracle. '[N]o theory of knowledge', he says, 'should attempt to explain why we are successful in our attempts to explain things' (1972, 23). And even though 'science has been miraculously successful,' as he puts it, '[t]his strange

3

fact cannot be explained' (*ibid.*, 204). Consistency with his other views requires him, no doubt, to disavow any presupposition that a scientific theory is likely to be true. Yet explanations of the success of science often make that very assumption: a theory's *success* is explained by assuming that the theory is *true*. Hence Popper's quandary. But throwing up our hands in despair or embracing miracles seem neither the heroic nor the reasonable thing to do. I have nothing heroic to offer by way of accounting for the success of science either, but I shall try a moderately reasonable stab at it.

Before proceeding further, something should be said about the term 'success'. There are several ways in which science is an overachiever. Its technological accomplishments are undeniable: it is very handy for building bridges and curing diseases. It is also a glorious entertainer: many of us would rather curl up in bed with a good piece of popular physics than with any novel. And science has also been a great success at extracting tax dollars from us all. (I do not say that cynically; I would gladly pay more.)

By calling science successful I do not mean that everything that is called science is successful, only that many current theories are. And by calling these theories successful I chiefly mean that:

1 they are able to organize and unify a great variety of known phenomena;
2 this ability to systematize the empirical data is more extensive now than it was for previous theories; and
3 a statistically significant number of novel predictions pan out, i.e. our theories get more predictions right than mere guessing would allow.

This, I think, is roughly what is involved in the normal use of the phrase 'the success of science', and I simply follow tradition here. At any rate these are the senses of success that I shall be dealing with. Even though they are common ingredients, they are not, however, always clearly distinguished by writers on this topic.

MIRACLES, DARWIN AND 'THE TRUTH'

The thing to be explained is the success of science, and the way realists often explain this fact is by claiming that theories are true, or at least approximately true, and that any conclusion deduced from true premisses must itself be true. So the assumption that theories are (approximately) true explains the success of those theories. Realism, as Hilary Putnam (1975a) puts it, is the only explanation which does not make the success of science a miracle. J. J. C. Smart states the case this way:

> If the phenomenalist about theoretical entities is correct, we must believe in a *cosmic coincidence*. That is, if this is so, statements about electrons, etc., are of only instrumental value: they simply enable us to predict phenomena on the level of galvanometers and cloud chambers. They do nothing to remove the *surprising character* of these phenomena. . . . Is it not odd that the phenomena of the world should be such as to make a purely instrumental theory true? On the other hand, if we interpret a theory in a realist way, then we have no need for such a cosmic coincidence: it is not surprising that galvanometers and cloud chambers behave in the sort of way they do, for if there really are electrons, etc., this is just what we should expect. A lot of surprising facts no longer seem surprising.
>
> (1968, 39)

We can reconstruct the argument in this passage in a way that makes it seem quite reasonable and convincing.

1 Conclusion O (an observation statement) can be *deduced* from theory T.
2 O is seen to be the case.
3 If T is true then the argument for O is *sound* and so O *had* to be true.
4 If T is false then the argument for O is *merely valid* and the probability of the arbitrary consequence O being true is very small (i.e. it would be a miracle if O were true).
5 Therefore the argument for O is probably sound.
6 Therefore T is probably true. (That is, even T's theoretical statements are probably true.)

This argument uses the realist's explanation of the success of science to draw ontological morals. Let us contrast it with a rival 'Darwinian' view of the anti-realist Bas van Fraassen, perhaps the most influential of recent anti-realists, who gives such an account of the success of science in *The Scientific Image*.[1] The explanation goes something like this: just as there are a great many species struggling for existence, so too have a great many theories been proposed. But just as species which are not adapted to their environment become extinct, so too are theories which do not make true observational predictions dropped. The belief that our theories might be true, or even approximately true, is therefore an illusion. It is similar to the illusion that Darwin undermined, that species are evolving *toward some goal*. van Fraassen writes:

> I can best make the point by contrasting two accounts of the mouse who runs from its enemy, the cat. St. Augustine . . . provided an intensional explanation: the mouse *perceives that* the cat is its enemy, hence the mouse runs. What is postulated here is the 'adequacy' of the mouse's thought to the order of nature: the relation of enmity is correctly reflected in his mind. But the Darwinist says: Do not ask why the *mouse* runs from its enemy. Species which did not cope with their natural enemies no longer exist. That is why there are only ones who do.

And so, he continues:

> In just the same way, I claim that the success of current scientific theories is no miracle. It is not even surprising to the scientific (Darwinist) mind. For any scientific theory is born into a life of fierce competition, a jungle red in tooth and claw. Only the successful theories survive – the ones which *in fact* latched on to actual regularities in nature.
>
> (1980, 39f)

'Truth' plays no role at all in the success of science for the Darwinian anti-realist. Yet for the realist it is the central explanatory factor. So here we have two main contenders, but could either of these explanations of the success of science be right?

THE DARWINIAN ANSWER

I characterized the success of science as having three ingredients. Van Fraassen's Darwinian explanation seems to account for two of these features, but not the third. He has an apparently adequate answer to the questions why theories get so much right and why newer theories get more right than the ones we have tossed out. The simple answer is that we have tossed out any theory which did not organize, unify and generally get a lot right; and we have tossed out theories which have done less well, comparatively, than others.

However, the third question is still unanswered. Why do our theories make correct predictions more often than one could expect on the basis of mere chance? Here the Darwinian analogy breaks down since most species could not survive a radical change of environment, the analogue of a novel prediction.

There is also a more general problem with van Fraassen's Darwinian approach. It is a problem which stems from the empiricism of anti-realists. An implicit assumption is that rational choice and success go hand in hand. On this assumption it is not surprising that science is successful in the senses (1) and (2) given on page 4, since we choose theories, says the empiricist, on that very basis. This, I think, is not so. Success, as characterized by a van Fraassen-type anti-realist, is a totally empirical notion. But in reality theories are rationally evaluated on the basis of several other considerations besides empirical factors. I do not wish to argue here for any in particular, but let us suppose that conceptual, metaphysical and aesthetic concerns play a role in actual theory choice. (van Fraassen calls these 'pragmatics' and allows that they play a role.) Consequently, it is *not* a trivial analytic truth that the rational thing to believe is also the most successful (as success was characterized above). Anyone who is not an extreme empiricist must concede that it is quite *possible* that the most rationally acceptable theory is not the most successful theory.

So even the Darwinian answers to (1) and (2) which above I tentatively conceded to be adequate are, in fact, not adequate after all. And (3), of course, remains entirely unexplained. The Darwinian account, linked to an empiricist methodology, yields a plausible account of two of the three aspects of success, but unlinked from this untenable methodology it accounts for nothing.

REALISM AND REFERENCE

A belief common to scientific realists is that the succession of theories is getting closer to the truth. This belief may well be true (I hope it is), but it is often tied to a doctrine that says that the central terms of one theory refer to the same things as the central terms of its successor and predecessor theories. Moreover, the intuitive idea of getting-closer-to-the-truth will itself need fleshing out in the form of an explicit doctrine of verisimilitude. Unfortunately, there are terrible problems with both of these. Beliefs about the constancy of reference run afoul of the history of science, and the concept of verisimilitude is plagued with technical problems. Even a cursory glance at the past suggests that there is no royal road to the truth such as that implied by the convergence picture, and every explication of verisimilitude so far proposed has been a crashing failure. Let's look at things now in some detail. In the most quoted version of the realist's explanation of the success of science, Putnam writes:

> The positive argument for realism is that it is the only philosophy that doesn't make the success of science a miracle. That terms in mature theories typically refer (this formulation is due to Richard Boyd), that the theories accepted in a mature science are typically approximately true, that the same term can refer to the same thing even when it occurs in different theories – these statements are viewed by the scientific realist not as necessary truths but as part of the only scientific explanation of the success of science, and hence as part of any adequate scientific description of science and its relations to its objects.
>
> (1975a, 73)

In the next section I shall examine the idea that mature theories are 'typically approximately true' by looking at Newton-Smith's views, since they are much more developed than Putnam's. This section will be devoted solely to examining the claim that 'terms in mature theories typically refer'. Let us begin by looking at a very simple theory:

Alasdair loves Hegel.

For the sake of the argument, let us suppose that it is quite a successful theory (there were reports of his buying several works by Hegel, waxing eloquent about Hegel's logic, hanging a picture of Hegel on his office wall etc.) and that all the terms in this simple theory refer. But is the fact that all the terms refer *sufficient* to explain why the theory is successful? The simplest consideration completely undermines this supposition. The following theory, we may suppose, is very unsuccessful:

Alasdair does *not* love Hegel.

Yet all the relevant terms just as surely refer.

Not all counter-examples are so artificial; historical illustrations of the problem abound. Consider the succession of atomistic theories; some were successful, but many were not. So clearly, having the term 'atom' in the theory does not lead to success even though (we believe) the term 'atom' refers.

Reference is not *sufficient* for success, but is it *necessary*? This, too, seems most unlikely. Phlogiston theories, caloric theories, aether theories and numerous others have all had a definite heyday; yet, by our present best guesses, the central terms of these theories do not refer. In the Putnam–Boyd explanation of the success of science there is a caveat. The term 'typically' is used: 'terms typically refer' and theories are 'typically approximately true'. This seems to leave one free to dismiss the occasional example such as phlogiston or caloric as a tolerable aberration. It would then appear to be a question of degree, and consequently the historical case for or against this sort of realism is going to be rather difficult to establish.

One could seriously doubt that the historical cases will come out the way Putnam and Boyd expect, i.e. with successful theories *typically* having terms which refer. But even if this should be the case with almost every theory, there still remains one great problem. A *single* example of a successful theory with at least one central term which does not refer must count as a miracle. Thus, the success of the caloric theory of heat, by the lights of Putnam and Boyd, must rank with the raising of Lazarus from the dead; and what Priestley achieved with his phlogiston theory was no less an amazing feat than if he had turned water into wine.

By weakening the claim to just saying that reference is *typical*, easy counter-examples drawn from the history of science might be avoided. But the cost is impossibly high – every atypical example is a miracle.

REALISM AND VERISIMILITUDE

It is time now to look at the other key idea in the Putnam–Boyd explanation of the success of science, the idea that theories are 'typically approximately true'. Unfortunately, neither Putnam nor Boyd has bothered to unpack this notion, so I shall examine the similar but rather more developed views of William Newton-Smith instead.

Newton-Smith's approach to verisimilitude is a 'transcendental' one as he puts it. He too is looking for an explanation of what he sees is an undeniable fact: *science has made progress*. And how has this remarkable achievement come about? His realist answer is disarmingly simple: if our theories were getting closer to the truth then this is exactly what we should expect (1981, 196).

To maintain a doctrine of increasing *verisimilitude*, or truth-likeness, is to maintain that the succession of past theories, up to the present, has been getting *closer to the truth*. There may be several respects in which later theories are better than earlier ones; they may be better predictors, more elegant, technologically more fruitful. But the one respect the realist cares about most is veracity; later theories, it is hoped and claimed, are better in this regard. Verisimilitude is an intuitive notion to which most people subscribe; but it is extremely problematic. The most famous instance of trying to come to grips with it, namely Popper's account (1972), is a clear-cut failure. And unless someone is able to successfully explicate the notion soon, it is likely to have the same fate as such other intuitive notions as 'neutral observation' and 'simplicity' – it will be tossed on the junk pile of history.

There is one virtue of Newton-Smith's account of verisimilitude which needs to be stressed. Constancy of reference across successive theories is not required. The kind of problems phlogiston, caloric and the aether present for the convergence account of Putnam and Boyd have no bearing on Newton-Smith's version. This is what makes his account interesting, initially promising and worthy of special attention.

Let me now focus on some of the details. What is required, as Newton-Smith sees it (1981, 198), is an analysis of the notion which will then justify the crucial premiss in his argument. That is, he must show that, on unpacking, the concept of verisimilitude yields this: an increase in verisimilitude implies the likeliness of an increase in observational success. And he is quite right to worry about this, for in spite of its intuitive nature, we cannot count on the properties of *truth* carrying over to *truthlikeness*. The consequences of a true theory must be true, but the consequences of a theory which is approximately true need not themselves be approximately true.

Before getting to his analysis of verisimilitude, we need to set the stage with Newton-Smith's characterization of a few key notions. A *theory* is the deductive closure of the postulates and appropriate auxiliary hypotheses; an *observational consequence* is a conditional, $p \rightarrow q$, where p is a statement of the observable initial conditions and q the observable final conditions; the consequences of a theory must be *recursively enumerable* (i.e. mechanically producible in a sequence – Newton-Smith does not defend this dubious condition). A theory *decides* p if it implies either p or its negation. The *content* of a theory is a fairly technical notion, but we can say roughly that one theory has more content than another if it decides more sentences. Since typically both will decide infinitely many sentences some technical complications in the definition are required. Imagine two theories, T_1 and T_2, with their consequences recursively enumerated. The nth member of the sequence generated from T_1 either will or will not be decided by T_2. We are to determine which it is. (Given Church's theorem, this is not going to be mechanically possible.) This process is generalized and finally we are able to form the appropriate ratio from the sentences decided by the two theories. In this way Newton-Smith is able to define which theory has the greater content, and he is able to do so in a manner which seems to capture our intuitive requirements. Of course, the definition is based on an infinite sequence, but for practical purposes greater content could be determined after a large, but finite, number of sentences have been examined.

The last important notion is that of *relative truth*. Consider again the theories T_1 and T_2 with their consequences enumerated recursively. After n terms there will be a number of truths and a number of falsehoods for each. The ratio of these numbers is the *truth ratio*. We then pick a third theory, T_3, to appraise the truth values of the sentences in the sequence generated by T_1 and T_2. (T_3 could be either from a God's eye point of view or it

11

could be our presently held theory.) Newton-Smith then defines T_2 as having *greater truth relative to* T_3 than T_1 has, if and only if the infinite sequence of ratios, which give the ratio of truths in T_1 to the truths in T_2 as judged by reference to T_3, has a limit greater than $\frac{1}{2}$. Now we come to the main idea:

T_2 has greater *verisimilitude* than T_1 if and only if both:
(1) the relative content of T_2 is equal to or greater than T_1.
(2) T_2 has greater truth relative to T_3 than T_1.

(1981, 204)

So the rough idea is this: to have more verisimilitude is, first, to say more about the world and, second, to say more true things in doing so. Does this solve the initial problem which was to show that greater verisimilitude implied the likelihood of greater observational success? The answer, says Newton-Smith, is yes. Here is his argument: pick an arbitrary sentence from T_2 which we shall assume has greater verisimilitude than T_1 according to our definition. The chances of it being true, since it came from T_2, are greater than the chances of some arbitrary sentence which comes from T_1 being true. And since the set of arbitrary sentences of T_2 includes the observational sentences it follows that T_2 will likely have more observational successes.

Newton-Smith's account of the notion of truth-likeness certainly has its attractions. It is not obviously plagued with the same problems which beset Popper's account; it is simple and elegant; and it satisfies several of our most basic intuitions about the concept. However, it still seems to be not entirely satisfactory, as a number of considerations show.

Is Newton-Smith's explanation good at accounting for all three senses of success (see page 4)? Not entirely. It is very good at accounting for (2) (theories explain more now than in the past). But it doesn't say why present theories get much right. It is perfectly compatible with Newton-Smith's theory that our present beliefs organize the data poorly, make few successful novel predictions and generally get very little right. His theory guarantees that our present scientific theories do better than our past theories. But there are important senses of success left unexplained.

Another problem that I see with Newton-Smith concerns a theory's content. Historical considerations make his requirement of increasing content in the definition of greater verisimilitude implausible. Any event in the history of science where the domain shrank – and there are several of them – will stand as a counter-example. Newton-Smith's requirement is that the later theory must have equal or greater content than the former. But this did not happen in the following example which most of us would probably consider a progressive move: once there were theories which combined astronomy and astrology together; then a transition was made to purely astronomical theories. The earlier theories which combined both astronomical and astrological claims obviously said more about the world, so the later astronomical theories had less content. However we characterize truth-likeness, it must be compatible with such domain shrinking transitions in the history of science. Newton-Smith's account is not.

IS HYPOTHETICO-DEDUCTIVISM THE PROBLEM?

What about the style of Newton-Smith's argument which links greater verisimilitude with the likelihood of greater observational success? Anti-realists often decry the hypothetico-deductive (H-D) form of inference. That is, they reject arguments which go:

Theory → Observation
Observation
∴ (Probably) Theory

Given that they find H-D arguments unconvincing (claiming that it is a simple fallacy of affirming the consequent), why should anti-realists be persuaded to become realists by an argument that goes: verisimilitude would explain greater observational success and there has been greater observational success; thus, there must be greater verisimilitude? The style is the same in both cases:

Greater verisimilitude → Greater observational success
Greater observational success
∴ (Probably) Greater verisimilitude

The anti-realist will simply say that the question has been begged. Some of us may like Newton-Smith's argument for verisimilitude and the realist approach in general, but then we *already* liked H-D inference. Laudan, however, gives voice to the anti-realist sentiment when he writes:

13

Ever since antiquity critics of epistemic realism have based their scepticism upon a deep-rooted conviction that the fallacy of affirming the consequent is indeed fallacious. . . . Now enters the new breed of realist . . . who wants to argue that epistemic realism can reasonably be presumed to be true by virtue of the fact that it has true consequences. But this is a monumental case of begging the question.

(1981, 45)

Can the blame for the failures to explain the success of science be pinned on H-D inference? At first glance the fight between realists and anti-realists over the success of science seems but a dressed up version of the old problem of induction. If there is no hope of solving that problem, then how can we hope to explain the success of science? The answer, I think, is that they are not really the same problem. If H-D reasoning were really the issue here it would be a problem for anti-realists, too. But van Fraassen, a paradigm anti-realist, relies on H-D inference regularly, as he must, for instance, in the following type of argument.

T is empirically adequate → Observation O
Observation O
∴ (Probably) T is empirically adequate

Van Fraassen wants to go as little beyond the observable evidence as he can, but he does take some risks. He resists inferences to the truth but in accepting a theory as empirically adequate he recognizes the need for ampliative inference.

Similarly, Laudan, when he has on his historian's hat, says the shift to the H-D style of inference with Hartley and LeSage was a step forward in the history of methodology (see, for example, Laudan 1977). Before their work, the Newtonian tradition of doing science was associated with the famous dictum, *hypothesis non fingo*; theories were to be deduced from the phenomena. The introduction of H-D in the eighteenth century marked a definite advance, says Laudan, and most would concur (though some recent readings of Newton would dispute this – see Harper 1990).

Anti-realists such as van Fraassen and Laudan are not *sceptics* about induction. They need and use inductive inference as much as realists do. If realists are committing a fallacy at the meta-level of explaining science, then so is everyone else (except perhaps Popper) at the theory level of explaining the world. But to give up inductive inference entirely, which neither realists nor anti-realists wish to do, is just to stop doing science altogether.

There is, in fact, a range of possibilities here where one might be tempted to draw a line. Consider the following:

I   Evidence E is true
II   Theory T is empirically adequate
III The entities T posits exist
IV   T is true

They are ordered in terms of decreasing probability, given evidence E. An inductive sceptic will, of course, accept E given E, but will go no further. Van Fraassen will accept the likes of II, given E, but resists III and IV. The niche between II and IV is interesting, though not common. Ian Hacking (1983) holds something like it with his realism based on experimental manipulation and Nancy Cartwright (1983) believes that there are electrons but that the electron theory is false. Her half realist–half anti-realist view is partly revealed in her provocative title *How the Laws of Physics Lie*.[2] The full-blooded realist is prepared in principle to accept IV. All of this makes it clear that there are anti-realist positions between full realism and inductive scepticism. The fight, contrary to Laudan, is not over the legitimacy of induction, but when and where to use it. Laudan is not alone; Arthur Fine picks up on the same point.

FINE'S ONTOLOGICAL ATTITUDE

Arthur Fine's 'The natural ontological attitude' has been an influential and much discussed paper since it appeared in the middle of the debate about scientific realism. NOA, as he calls it, simply accepts the assertions of science at face value. It is not a brand of realism; 'And not anti-realism either', as the title of a follow-up paper announces. Fine's idea would seem to be that the common-sense reading of scientific assertions is the right one. But if this is so, why then are realists being attacked by Fine? Isn't this exactly what realists hold? Clearly it is; realism has only become an explicit doctrine because of the attack on it by anti-realists. I take realism to be just a reflective attempt to defend the 'natural', unreflective, common-sensical reading of the assertions of science.

Perhaps all that NOA comes to is realism *without* a defence. In other words, any argument for NOA would perhaps be an argument for realism. It is hard to say, since NOA is not spelled out or directly argued for; Fine criticizes realists and anti-realists, then NOA 'wins' by default. I'm inclined to see NOA as less the formulation of an ontological point of view than the ventilation of impatience with a perennial philosophical problem.

For the most part the NOA paper is a sustained attack on realists. One of Fine's chief targets is the no-miracles argument. As we have just seen, anti-realists have strong doubts about the inference: T is a good explanation, therefore T is (probably) true. Given these reservations it would seem (for them) to be a case of begging the question when a realist says: approximate truth is a good explanation of success, so we should accept the truth of that explanation (i.e. our theories are approximately true). But, as was suggested above, there is another way to look at things. Realists could say they are simply modelling their argument on a form that any anti-realist (who is not a complete sceptic) would accept. Again, let's make this explicit:

I   T is empirically adequate → Observation O
     Observation O
     ∴ T is empirically adequate

II   T is approximately true → T is successful
     T is successful
     ∴ T is approximately true

(In realistic situations background assumptions will play a role making inferences more complex and subtle than represented here. But we can ignore this since it is the similarity between I and II which is at issue.) Anti-realists make ampliative inferences of the same form as the success argument. Of course, it is not deductively valid, but if it is an inductive *fallacy* then everyone is making it all over the place. Fine, however, won't let all of us make it. He demands more stringent standards for philosophy than for science. Inference forms such as the above are legitimate, perhaps, when they concern empirical adequacy, but not when they concern truth. But why?

Hilbert's programme serves as a model for Fine: mathematics

is allowed infinitary methods, but meta-mathematics may only employ finitary techniques. 'Hilbert's maxim applies to the debate over realism: to argue for realism one must employ methods more stringent than those in ordinary scientific practice' (1986, 115).

It is an interesting analogy, but Fine misuses it. He says of Hilbert's programme that anything short of stricter standards is worthless. But this is a false dichotomy: a proof of the consistency of mathematics is either finitary *or* completely worthless. (By analogy, any argument is either a non-inductive argument for realism or else is totally illegitimate.) This overlooks Gentzen's non-finitistic proof of the consistency of arithmetic which was a great achievement. True, his technique was as 'dubious' as the number theory he set out to legitimize, but the fact that he succeeded in making the whole fit together better than before must surely increase our confidence in that whole. Gentzen's proof does not increase our confidence greatly, but its impact is not negligible either. This, I think, is how we should understand explanations of the success of science which use approximate truth.

Let me put the Gentzen point the other way around. Suppose that he had proved something quite different, an extension of Gödel's incompleteness result, to the effect that there is no infinitary proof of the consistency of mathematics either. If Gentzen had actually proved this, our faith in the consistency of classical mathematics might reasonably decline. So if such a negative result could lead to such an attitude, then Gentzen's actual positive result must surely be taken as lending support to the belief that arithmetic is indeed consistent. Analogously, suppose we had some sort of meta-argument that there could not be a success of science argument concluding that our theories are (approximately) true. Our faith in realism would be shattered. So, given that we have such an argument, shouldn't our faith in realism be at least slightly reinforced?

Attempts such as Fine's to shrug off the realism–anti-realism debate are likely to be unsuccessful. Consider an analogous situation outside of science, say in theology. The analogue of NOA would be to take the Bible at face value. This we might imagine to be done by all until it is pointed out that certain geological and biological facts are incompatible with Genesis. Some conclude from this evidence that the Bible is false; these are the atheists. Fundamentalists hold to its truth, and deny the alleged facts of science. There is, of course, yet a third position which stems from the debate so far. It holds that the Bible is indeed true, but should not be read literally. Atheists and fundamentalists, in reaction to the non-literal reading of the Bible, become explicit realists in theology (where realism means the statements of theology are literally true or literally false); the so-called liberal theologians are the anti-realists. These rival philosophical views inevitably arise and displace the unreflective 'natural' reading of the Bible. NOA is the initial outlook – in science or theology – but it cannot be the final one.

WHY TRUTH MATTERS (A LITTLE)

It is now time to take stock. By explaining success, remember, there are three things to be accounted for: (1) that our current theories organize, unify and generally account for a wide variety of phenomena; (2) that theories have been getting better and better at this, they are progressing; and (3) that a significant number of their novel predictions are true. It is now time to stand back and see to where we have reached.

The debate concerning this attempt to account for the success of science is not just a re-enactment of the problem of induction. So there is perhaps some hope of coming up with an answer. Realist explanations of success may well beg the question against that age old problem, but then we all (including the anti-realists) do that all the time. Induction, in principle, is not what is at issue here; rather it is a *particular* inference that is being debated.

Van Fraassen's account has no answer at all for (3), i.e. for the fact that theories make novel predictions which are found to be true. It has an explanation of (1), the significant degree of empirical adequacy, and (2), the increasing degree of empirical adequacy over time, but it can explain these only by linking rational theory choice to success *by definition*. Since this is methodologically implausible, even his explanations of (1) and (2) are thus not acceptable.

Let us turn now to the realist's account of things. Explaining the second aspect of success (theories are getting better) is probably the most popular approach. Leplin (1980) thinks it is the most promising and Newton-Smith, as we saw earlier, builds his doctrine of verisimilitude around it. Actually, it may be the least promising. Some realist explanations of this sense of the success of science quite explicitly need a theory of verisimilitude. However, none seems available. Newton-Smith was criticized above and other versions of the doctrine have not gone unscathed either. The historical record makes the prospects for one look rather dim; verisimilitude may have to go the way of, say, 'simplicity'.

The third sense of success (novel predictions) seems also to be promising for the realist. Predictions about the future which turn out to be true are not just lucky guesses on the realist's account. These predictions are deduced from the truth, says the realist; so it is no wonder that the 'guesses' panned out. There is no rival explanation for this; the Darwinian explanation of van Fraassen didn't even try to account for it. In Laudan's very detailed attack on convergent realism (1981) there is very little mention of this sense of success. So it remains something to which the realist might point as a genuine accomplishment, something to which the anti-realist fails to do justice. But how strong is this? How much support does this give to the realist? Unfortunately, many theories now thought to be false made true novel predictions. Ptolemaic astronomy, for instance, predicted eclipses fairly accurately. And Fresnel rather surprisingly got right his prediction of a bright spot in the middle of a shadow cast by a disk. So being true is hardly necessary for making successful predictions.

It is hard to say why realist accounts of the success of science have gone wrong. Of course, one answer is that realism itself is wrong. But this is an answer we should be loath to accept; so before we do, let's explore at least one different kind of approach to the problem. What realists need, I suggest, is a different style of explanation entirely. I shall now try to spell this out, if only briefly. I stress the tentative, exploratory and sketchy nature of the proposal to follow; it is intended merely as a beginning.

The last four decades have seen considerable quarrelling over the form of a proper explanation. The dominant theory has been the so-called deductive-nomological or covering law model proposed by Hempel (see Hempel 1965). For probabilistic situations there is the so-called inductive-statistical account. Either way, on Hempel's view, an explanation is an argument. Given the explanans, the explanandum is shown to have been expected. (In the deductive case it is certainly expected and in the inductive case the explanandum is expected with high probability.) In short, an explanation is a sufficient or almost sufficient condition for what is being explained.

Here lies the difficulty. The preceding considerations show that truth is neither a necessary nor a sufficient condition for the success of science. It does not meet the Hempelian conditions at all. Since it is not even close to being sufficient in any probabilistic sense we cannot subsume it under the inductive-statistical version of the covering law model either. But the idea that it might have something to do with statistical considerations is, perhaps, an idea worth exploring.

Wesley Salmon proposed[3] an account of explanation which rivals the covering law account of Hempel. An explanation is not an argument for a conclusion; it is instead the marshalling of the statistically relevant facts which have a bearing on the outcome. His view was introduced to cope with examples such as this: 'Why does Jones have paresis?' Explanation: 'Because he had syphilis.' This seems intuitively like a good explanation, yet the outcome, Jones's paresis, is not likely at all. The chances of getting paresis are very small with syphilis, but larger than they would be without it. Having syphilis, says Salmon, is statistically relevant; that is why it explains Jones's paresis. (A is statistically relevant to B if and only if Prob(B, given A) $\neq$ Prob(B).)[4]

We know that false premises can yield true conclusions, so truth is not (logically speaking) necessary for success. The reason truth is not sufficient for success is because of the presence of auxiliary assumptions which are also at work in any explanation. However, even though truth is neither sufficient nor necessary for success, it is, I shall say following Salmon, statistically relevant. The truth matters to the outcome, though it only matters a little. But it is not any statistical account of explanation that I really care to embrace. Instead, I mention it here only as a kind of introduction to another explanatory form, one which I do want to adopt for explaining the success of science.

NARRATIVE EXPLANATIONS

Salmon's statistical relevance model is not the only challenger to the Hempelian account. Some philosophers of biology and other philosophers of history[5] have advocated a *narrative* style of explanation. An event or condition is explained by telling a story in which the thing to be explained is embedded. In this way the explanandum is said to be rendered 'intelligible'; from the story we see how the events in question are possible. It is often claimed that Darwinian evolution, for instance, is unable to satisfy the Hempelian form, but that it is explanatory nevertheless. It provides neither necessary nor sufficient conditions, but it succeeds in some sense or other in explaining things.

Consider some examples: Why does the giraffe have a long neck? Explanation: The ancestors of the modern giraffe fed on trees, and those with long necks were able to reach more when food was scarce (such as in the occasional drought). There would have been some survival value in having a long neck, so there was, consequently, differential selection in its favour.

Is this meant by the evolutionist to be true? Not with any degree of confidence. It is only meant to be an evolutionary *possibility*, one of the many courses (within the Darwinian framework) that nature *might* have taken.

Let's turn to thought experiments for a second example. These marvellous devices work in a variety of ways; one type shows how something is possible. In the nineteenth century James Clerk Maxwell was a champion of the molecular-kinetic theory of heat (Maxwell 1871) which says that a gas is a collection of molecules in rapid random motion obeying Newton's laws. In this theory where things are treated statistically, temperature is just the average kinetic energy of the molecules, pressure is due to the molecules hitting the walls of the container etc. A successful statistical theory of heat must imply the second law of thermodynamics, the law that requires the entropy to remain the same or increase in any change of state. Equivalently, heat cannot pass from a cold to a hot body. But the best any statistical law of entropy can do is make the decrease of entropy very improbable. Thus, on Maxwell's theory there is some chance (though very small) that heat would flow from a cold body to a hot body when brought into contact, something which has never been experienced and which is absolutely

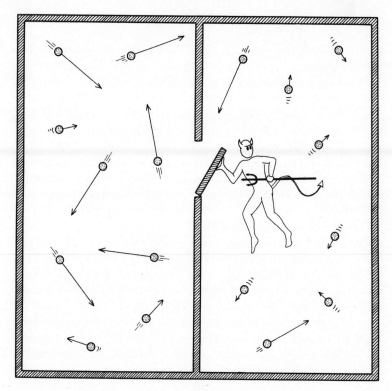

Figure 1

forbidden by classical thermodynamics. Is this an outright absurdity, something like an energy-producing perpetual motion machine?

Imagine two gases in separate chambers brought together; there is a little door between the two containers and a little intelligent being who controls the door (Figure 1). Even though the average molecule in the hot gas is faster that the average in the cold, there is a distribution of molecules at various speeds in each chamber. The demon lets fast molecules from the cold gas into the hot chamber and slow molecules from the hot gas into the cold chamber. The demon thought experiment was Maxwell's attempt to make the possible decrease of entropy in his theory not seem so obviously absurd. The demon's actions *increase* the average speed of the molecules in the hot chamber and *decrease* the average speed in the cold one, making the hot

22

gas hotter and the cold gas colder. This, of course, violates the second law of classical thermodynamics.

The point of the whole exercise is to show that what was unthinkable is not so unthinkable after all; it is, we see on reflection, not an objection to Maxwell's version of the second law that it is statistical and allows the possibility of a decrease in entropy. Maxwell's demon helps to make some of the conclusions of the theory more plausible; it removes a barrier to its acceptance. It shows how something is possible after all.

Now let's turn back to realism. My suggestion is that realism works as an explanation for the success of science in the same way as the demon thought experiment explains how entropy can decrease and in the same way as the story about the possible history of giraffes explains how the long necks of current giraffes are possible in Darwin's theory. In each case they answer a 'How possible?' question – standard fare for any narrative explanation. The intrinsic plausibility of the answer itself is not at issue. The explanation (within the Darwinian framework) of the giraffe's long neck is quite plausible. On the other hand, the demon is intrinsically implausible. But in neither case does this matter; the point of these explanations is to let us see how the phenomenon in question could come about. And this is exactly what truth-as-the-explanation-for-the-success-of-science does. It lets us see how science could be successful.

In some respects narrative explanations are similar to statistical relevance explanations. Neither are guaranteed to provide necessary or sufficient conditions for what is being explained. What both do, however, is provide something which is relevant to the outcome. Yet, there is also a difference between them. The statistically relevant information in, for example, the Jones' paresis case is the *known* fact that Jones had syphilis. In typical narrative explanations the relevant fact in the explanation is not known to be true – it is conjectured. So, the realist has an explanation for the success of science: truth is the explanation and the style of the explanation is narrative. The truth is not known to obtain; it is conjectured. But even if it did obtain, success would not automatically follow. The presence of the truth, however, does make a difference; truth is relevant to the outcome.

The Hempel model of explanation is tied to confirmation. By

deducing the data from the theory, the theory explains the data and in turn the data confirm the theory. Alas, this is not the case here. Saying that a theory is true does not lead to any testable predictions over and above those already made by saying that the theory is empirically adequate. There is no additional predictive power to this sort of narrative explanation. But even though predictive power is lost, this does not lead to the demise of the claim to have explanatory power. We cannot predict why a radioactive atom decays at the precise moment that it does; but after it happens we can explain it. The fact that the quantum theory can give such *post hoc* explanations does count in its favour, though only very little. The explanatory power of truth is similar.

I just said quantum mechanics can 'explain' why an atom decays at some precise moment. Is this really true? It depends on what is meant by an 'explanation'. In one sense the answer is, clearly, no. According to (orthodox) quantum mechanics the world is irreducibly chancy; there is no cause for the atom's decay at that precise moment so there is no hope of describing a mechanism that made the event occur. If this is what is required of an explanation, then the decay cannot be explained. However, if a novice asks 'Why did the atom decay at that moment?', we can give a useful reply. We tell the novice about quantum mechanics, about how there was such-and-such a probability of decay and so on. At the end of this the novice is *enlightened*, i.e. understands what has happened. It is a completely full and satisfying explanation in the sense that the questioner now knows more than before and, indeed, knows everything there is to know about the event.

There are two types of quantum mechanical explanation. When we explain spectral lines or molecular structure using quantum mechanics, we explain in a traditional way, we derive the explanandum from the explanans. But when we explain the decay of an individual atom at some specific time, we embed the event in a big story which makes the event understandable. This is the narrative style so often used by historians and evolutionary biologists – and, say I, by realists who use truth to explain success.

In most explanations there is a connection to justification. That is why Popper does not want truth to explain success. But there are also explanations which are not linked to justification and that, I think, is what we have here. We show how, given realism, the success of science is possible, why it is not a miracle. But the narrative style of the explanation does not let us infer its correctness – we cannot count on the (approximate) truth of the theories at all.

Realism is a wonderfully rich and enlightening story – a true story, I think – which makes our thought and our experience intelligible. Anti-realism says our theories are 'tales . . . full of sound and fury, signifying nothing'. In the long run it may be possible to find convincing evidence for one of these accounts over the other. But for now we can only make a choice based on which story – realism or anti-realism – makes the most sense of things. I choose the realist story.

And the following chapters should all be seen in this light.

Part II

SMOKE

The realist picture of science has had numerous critics of late. The following four chapters fight back: first, against Rorty's ethnocentric solidarity view, next against Latour's 'anthropologist in the lab' account, then against Ruse's Darwinian epistemology, and finally against Putnam's recent verificationism. These chapters are mostly critical – but not entirely. Glimpses of an alternative account are also offered.

SMOKE

2

RORTY'S SOLIDARITY

Relativism is a repugnant doctrine – reprehensible, repulsive and easily refuted. But 'solidarity'? Richard Rorty has served up some old ideas in a new and attractive way. Instead of the tired old formula of 'truth is just true for us', Rorty has a different twist: objectivity gives way to *solidarity*. He 'would like to replace the desire for objectivity – the desire to be in touch with a reality which is more than some community with which we identify ourselves – with the desire for solidarity with that community' (1987, 39). For those of us who occasionally march to the tune of *Solidarity Forever*, it is hard to feel too grumpy about the picture Rorty paints. Solidarity just doesn't have the sense of selfishness about it that relativism does. Still, the underlying ideas are similar. Truth, for Rorty, is not something transcendent that we all search for – it is instead connected to the here and now, to the practices of particular communities.

UNFORCED AGREEMENT

Rorty intends his view to be completely general. Solidarity is the key whether we're talking about the everyday beliefs and political opinions of ordinary people or the most esoteric doctrines of particle physicists. There are social and moral aspects to each of these. Scientists, in particular, do not possess a 'method' for getting at the truth. Instead, says Rorty,

The habits of relying on persuasion rather than force, of respect for the opinions of colleagues, of curiosity and eagerness for new data and ideas, are the *only* virtues which scientists have . . . [There is no] intellectual virtue called 'rationality' over and above these moral virtues.

(*ibid.*)

For the most part Rorty is pretty deflationary. Those who dismiss the objectivity of science are typically out to discredit it, but this is not entirely so with Rorty – he finds one important feature to praise.

On this view there is no reason to praise scientists for being more 'objective' or 'logical' or 'methodological' or 'devoted to truth' than other people. But there is plenty of reason to praise the institutions they have developed and within which they work, and to use these as models for the rest of culture. For these institutions give concreteness and detail to the idea of 'unforced agreement.' Reference to such institutions fleshes out the idea of 'a free and open encounter'. . . .

(1987, 39)

Of course, 'unforced agreement' is not really and truly a virtue for Rorty – nothing is 'really and truly' anything. But given our historical situation, we can see it as a virtue and recommend its adoption more widely.

However, it seems to me that Rorty's proposal is doubly wrong. Wrong, of course, in that it denies the objectivity of science (but at this stage in the argument I'm merely begging the question in saying so). The second way in which it is wrong has to do with the utterly uncritical way in which Rorty accepts the idea of 'unforced agreement'. Far too many people have suffered at the hands of science to let this myth pass. Perhaps *males* have come to an unforced agreement in their thinking about female sexuality; perhaps *whites* have come to an unforced agreement about black intelligence; perhaps *the rich* have come to an unforced agreement in their opinions about how a democratic economy works; but none of this sham agreement should pass as a model of how our various social institutions *should* be run.

Are these unfair examples? When I think of science I tend to think of physics – perhaps Rorty does too. There 'unforced agreement' often seems genuine and admirable. People's interests with respect to class, race and gender don't interfere, for example, in debates about the stability of the proton or the mass of the neutrino. But Sandra Harding (1986) has rightly stressed that physics is probably untypical science. Most scientists work in either the social sciences or the biological and health sciences. Here 'unforced agreement' is not what Rorty thinks, and may even be non-existent. I need only mention 'sociobiology' to make the point. Rorty claims that 'the only sense in which science is exemplary is that it is a model of human solidarity' (1987, 39). It is anything but.

Realists admire what they see as the genuine successes of science and glory in its unlimited potential. But we are not for a minute committed to thinking everything done in the name of science is praiseworthy. Believing that there really is such a thing as rationality, we can point to particular cases of 'unforced agreement' and declare them bogus. That is, we can say, 'Even though there was universal agreement about X, they were all wrong'. This is something relativists will find hard to do, since they – unlike realists – deny there is anything which transcends that agreement.

Much of my disagreement with Rorty over science may stem from a deeper disagreement about politics. I see his view as being very conservative. It may be philosophically radical, but it implicitly defends the status quo. Rorty's historically embedded actors can tolerate some disagreement and still carry on 'the conversation'; but on a solidarity view, such as his, they cannot abide deep criticisms. Revolutionary alternatives – about the structure of space–time or the structure of society – cannot be taken seriously. 'We Western liberal intellectuals', Rorty remarks, 'should accept the fact that we have to start from where we are, and that this means that there are lots of views which we simply cannot take seriously' (1985, 29). This attitude – so wrong, morally and historically – stems from Rorty's inherent conservatism. It is tempting to paraphrase it as 'We white, middle-class, males are happy to stay put and to thumb our noses at other views'.

RUSSELL'S PROMISCUITY

Bertrand Russell was often condemned for his promiscuity – both sexual and intellectual. He was as often criticized for changing his beliefs as for changing his lovers. Let's leave his sexual mores aside and focus on epistemological ones. Russell would propose a theory; it would be criticized – often effectively; so Russell would drop his old theory and adopt another. Now, isn't this the very paradigm of rational behaviour and intellectual honesty? Why the complaints? Christians may pride themselves on steadfastly holding their beliefs through thick and thin, but what contemporary self-respecting scientists, Russell noted, would proudly cling to classical theories?

A cynical explanation of these complaints is possible. It might include such elements as these: after working so hard to understand a subject, and perhaps teach it, people don't like to see it undermined so quickly; or, Russell is a moving target who wouldn't sit still and be refuted. I want to offer a quite different type of explanation for the criticism of Russell.

What I suspect is that rationality is really a *group activity*, and that those who criticize Russell have some sort of dim recognition of this fact. By calling rationality a group activity I mean that individuals may play different roles in the search for knowledge. Rational theory choice, for instance, is not a matter of taking a theory to nature and putting it to the test. Rather, we take collections of theories to nature and we get a rank-ordering. Nature doesn't tell us that some theory is right or wrong; it only tells us that this theory is better than that one. It would then be idiotic to have all scientists accepting and working on the same theory, even if it is rightly judged to be the best at the time. Clearly, it would be better to have our resources (scarce though they are) spread over several rival theories.

In this context, individuals should be thought of as resources. We want some people working on this theory, some on that theory and so on. In this process we really don't care what any individual believes. The crucial point is only this: that each theory is getting developed, modified and articulated in the best way. We expect and need those working on any particular theory to see it through to the end, until it is overwhelmingly obvious that it is much better or much worse than its rivals. When Russell switched theories so fast and so often, there was, I suspect, a kind of subconscious resentment that he is letting the side down. Normally group rationality is served by two things: most of us are much slower than Russell at recognizing the relative strengths and weaknesses of various theories; and second, we are much more protective of our intellectual creations than he was – they're a bit like our children. Both of these factors are useful in inclining us to stick with a particular theory over a fairly long haul. Put less charitably, we are pig-headed dogmatists – and often it's a good thing.

If group rationality isn't individual rationality writ large, but has the quite different structure suggested here, then there is an important moral to be drawn. Rorty's 'unforced agreement' is the last thing we want. *We have better theories by having different theories.*

This bring us back to where we started – to Rorty's solidarity. We can see a kind of human solidarity at work in the way group rationality operates. But remember, group rationality requires different people working on different theories and holding different beliefs; in short, it requires reasoned disagreement. So, can Rorty's solidarity replace objective truth? Not for a moment.

KUHN

One of Rorty's favourite sources of support is Kuhn. Ever since *The Structure of Scientific Revolutions* was published in 1962 it has been a source of comfort for anti-realists. Kuhn's image of science is one of an activity which *creates* the world it attempts to describe. 'In learning a paradigm the scientist acquires theory, methods, and standards together, usually in an inextricable mixture' (1962/1970, 109) says Kuhn, famously in one place. And infamously in another, 'In a sense that I am unable to explicate further, the proponents of competing paradigms practice their trades in different worlds' (*ibid.*, 150). But Rorty also wants to pull another rabbit out of Kuhn's hat – ethnocentrism. It's one he cannot have. Kuhn's normal scientists work within a paradigm; there is a way they see the world and they seem incapable of seeing it differently. This much of Kuhn does indeed lend support to Rorty's view, but beyond this point the similarity breaks down. Kuhn's normal scientists sometimes encounter crisis periods; new paradigms arise; scientists drop one paradigm and adopt another; a revolution is carried out; and then the same scientists see things very differently. They are working in 'different worlds'. By contrast, Rorty's ethnocentric communities are not capable of such radical change in their beliefs. Perhaps they can slowly evolve from one theory to another, but they are far too conservative to change overnight.

While there is much to quarrel with in Kuhn's revolutionary

account, it has done much greater justice to the history of science – the history of belief – than Rorty's plodding and conservative ethnocentrism could possibly hope for.

FROM GOD TO GAUSS

There is a gripping metaphor used by many anti-realists: we can't get out of our own heads to stand back and compare our thoughts with reality. Rorty has been extremely effective in making realists look hopelessly naive in thinking they could do just that. It is impossible to step outside our skins, he typically remarks, and compare ourselves with something absolute. 'What we cannot do is rise above all human communities, actual and possible. We cannot find a skyhook which lifts us out of mere coherence – mere agreement – to something like "correspondence with reality as it is in itself" ' (1987, 38). There is no God's-eye-point-of-view, and even if there were, we couldn't have it.

Realists (even atheists like me) often use the 'God's-eye-view' metaphor, but Rorty claims that realists must not only believe in a God's-eye-view, but believe in God, too.

> The suggestion that truth, as well as the world, is out there is a legacy of an age in which the world was seen as the creation of a being who had a language of his own.
>
> (1989, 5)

> The very idea that the world or the self has an intrinsic nature – one which the physicist or the poet may have glimpsed – is a remnant of the idea that the world is a divine creation, the work of someone who had something in mind, who Himself spoke some language in which He described His own project. Only if we have some such picture in mind, some picture of the universe as either itself a person or as created by a person, can we make sense of the idea that the world has an 'intrinsic nature'.
>
> (1989, 21)

This is exactly what realists do not believe. Of course, the dichotomy that Rorty sets up – his pragmatic anti-realism versus trying to talk God's language – is just a rhetorical device, designed to make realists look silly. Still, it is worth taking a moment to see why it's utterly wrong-headed.

The view Rorty pins on the realist is similar to one that says 'Without God there can be no morality', a view long ago refuted by Plato. In the *Euthyphro* we face the problem: Is something good because the gods say so, or do the gods say so because it is good? The former makes good and bad just a whim; the latter makes goodness independent of the gods. Plato rightly adopted the latter view, and so should we. When it comes to external reality we can ask a similar question: Is the world such and such *because God thinks it is*, or does God think the world is such and such *because it really is*? Obviously, contra Rorty, realists will hold the latter. (God may have created the world, but once created its properties are not dependent on God's *opinions* of what has been created.)

Realists would certainly be embarrassed by any link of their view to ghosts, goblins and God. Fortunately, Rorty has been unsuccessful in forging one. On the other hand, realists may have been a bit too ready to agree with the we-can't-get-out-of-our-skin-and-compare-our-thoughts-with-reality sentiment. By and large, this sentiment seems rather obvious, and we see the force of it as soon as it is pointed out. But it may just be false. Is there anything more than common sense to be said in its favour? Let me try a brief argument to the effect that we sometimes can get beyond our own thoughts to a reality beyond. It stems from Gauss's distinction between intrinsic and extrinsic geometry.

Suppose tiny, flat bugs live on a sheet of paper. There is no way they could determine whether their little universe is flat (Figure 2(a)) or curved (Figure 2(b)). With our extrinsic view, we can see which it is. Their two-dimensional world is embedded in our three-dimensional space. From this vantage point we have a 'God's-eye-view', *par excellence*.

But what if their two-dimensional world should be all that exists? Without a higher dimensional embedding space, would their two-dimensional space *really* be flat or *really* be curved? Or does the question no longer make sense? It is not merely a matter of their inability to verify which. For even when their world is embedded in ours, they cannot determine the curvature of their space, even though we (i.e. God) can. But when the embedding space is absent there seems no longer a fact of the matter to be either right or wrong about.

Now think about our own universe. Presumably it is a four-dimensional (space–time) manifold which is not embedded in

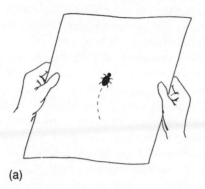

(a)

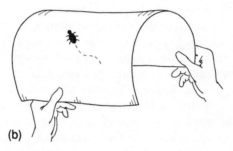

(b)

Figure 2 (a) Universe 1   (b) Universe 2

any higher dimensional space. There is no God's-eye-view. So, again, it would seem there is no sense to the question whether our space–time is really curved or really flat. Powerful ammunition for anti-realists.

Let's return to our little bugs, this time on a surface that resembles a hemisphere (Figure 3). The situation now is quite different from that in either Figure 2(a) or Figure 2(b). If bugs on this surface measured the interior angles of a triangle, they would discover that the sum is greater than 180 degrees. In both Figure 2(a) and Figure 2(b) the sum of interior angles in any triangle would always be 180 degrees, regardless of the curvature involved. What's the difference? Karl Fredrich Gauss ('The Prince of Mathematicians') distinguished *intrinsic* from *extrinsic* geometrical properties. Those properties which can be defined without reference to an embedding space are intrinsic; those which need the embedding space are extrinsic. What is now

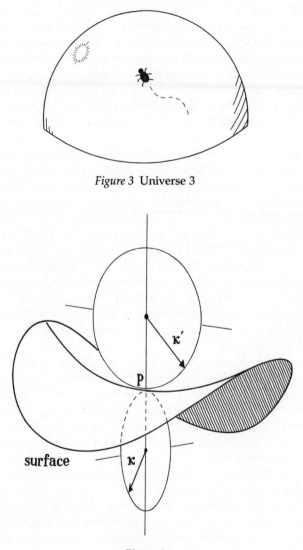

Figure 3 Universe 3

Figure 4

known as *Gaussian curvature* is an example of an intrinsic property. The Gaussian curvature of a surface at a point p is defined
as $1/\kappa\kappa'$, where κ and κ' are the radii of circles which would
touch at p – the curvature of the circles at that point matches (in
the limit) the curvature of the surface – and the circles are taken

in the x and y directions (Figure 4). Even though Gaussian curvature is defined with respect to a higher dimensional space than the surface is embedded within, it is nevertheless an intrinsic property of the surface, and one can determine its value *without* the need of an actual embedding space. Apply this to our three bug universes. A straight line is the same as the arc of a circle which has a radius that is infinitely large. So the flat sheet of paper (universe 1) has Gaussian curvature $1/(\infty \times \infty) = 0$. The curved sheet of paper (universe 2) has Gaussian curvature $1/(\infty \times r) = 0$, where r is the radius of curvature along one axis. Though these two spaces differ extrinsically, they have the same intrinsic curvature, namely, zero. The hemisphere (universe 3) is quite different. Supposing it to match a circle of radius r along both axes, its Gaussian curvature is $1/r^2 \neq 0$. This third little world is intrinsically different from the other two. To get a feel for this difference draw a triangle on a sheet of paper; hold it flat as in Figure 2(a); bend it as in Figure 2(b); note that the triangle is not distorted in any way by the bending; now try to wrap the sheet of paper around a basketball; it won't go without becoming distorted. What you see is the intrinsic equivalence of universes 1 and 2 and the intrinsic difference between them and universe 3.

This intrinsic difference can be measured from *within* the space. The bugs cannot distinguish between universes 1 and 2, since they both have Gaussian curvature zero; but they can measure triangles to determine whether they are in the set of universes which include 1 and 2, or instead in a universe like universe 3 which has non-zero Gaussian curvature. Once the bugs have determined this, they can conclude the following: if there is a higher dimensional space that their universe is embedded within, they can specify some of its extrinsic properties; and if there is no embedding space, they can still say what their universe would look like if such an embedding space did exist.

Here's the moral: The embedding space provides the God's-eye-view. If there is a God's-eye-view, the bugs can determine what it is; and if there is no God's-eye-view, the bugs can still say what such a view would be like if it did exist. And that's how Gauss gives us a God's-eye-view.

I realize that for a determined anti-realist this meta-theorizing is just more theorizing; perhaps we're not really comparing our thought with reality, just with more thought. Of course, all

dismissive talk of the God's-eye-view by anti-realists is meta-
phoric; and my use of Gauss is only this, as well. Nevertheless,
I'm willing to pit this sketchy argument against any other that
says we can never get outside to compare our thoughts with
reality. Of course, realism does not require that we be able to
'get outside our own heads'. It only maintains that there is a
thought-independent reality that our thought has some hope
of describing. Nevertheless, the-God's-eye-view-is-impossible
argument, though rhetorically quite effective, has really been
nothing but bluff and bluster.

ARGUMENTS AND PICTURES

Rorty's typical style of argument is to state in rather vague and
general terms some sweeping thesis; sometimes historical
figures (Plato, Descartes, Kant) are cited as wrong-doers; at
other times the view of an age is simply stated; then a number of
contemporaries (Heidegger, Wittgenstein, Davidson) are cited
as undermining the old guard; a synoptic history of the issue is
presented; and finally an equally sweeping conclusion is drawn.
Here is a characteristic example:

> Contemporary intellectuals have given up the Enlighten-
> ment assumption that religion, myth, and tradition can be
> opposed to something ahistorical, something common to
> all human beings qua human. Anthropologists and histor-
> ians of science have blurred the distinction between innate
> rationality and the products of acculturation. Philosophers
> such as Heidegger and Gadamer have given us ways of
> seeing human beings as historical all the way through.
> Other philosophers, such as Quine and Davidson, have
> blurred the distinction between permanent truths of
> reason and temporary truths of fact. . . .
> The effect of erasing this picture is to break the link
> between truth and justifiability.
>
> (1988b, 176)

As arguments go for Rorty, this is as rigorous as it usually gets.
We could easily complain, first, about the premises: perhaps
some intellectuals 'have given up the Enlightenment . . .', but
lots of others haven't; and being either 'permanent' or 'tempor-
ary' has nothing to do with the distinction between truths of

reason and truths of fact. Second, we could complain about the jump to this conclusion. Even if the premises were correct, it is still a million miles to this finale. How does Rorty get there?

But perhaps it is wrong to complain this way. The mistake is ours in thinking Rorty is playing our game – he's not. We should not expect Rorty to start with premises that we accept and lead us to surprising new conclusions. This way of doing philosophy is part and parcel of the very Enlightenment that he is at pains to reject.

> On the view of philosophy which I am offering, philos-ophers should not be asked for arguments against, for example, the correspondence theory of truth or the idea of the 'intrinsic nature of reality'. The trouble with arguments against the use of a familiar and time-honored vocabulary is that they are expected to be phrased in that very voca-bulary. They are expected to show that central elements in that vocabulary are 'inconsistent in their own terms' or that they 'deconstruct themselves'. But that can *never* be shown. Any argument to the effect that our familiar use of a familiar term is incoherent, or empty, or confused, or vague, or 'merely metaphorical' is bound to be inconclus-ive and question-begging. For such use is after all, the paradigm of coherent, meaningful, literal, speech. Such arguments are always parasitic upon, and abbreviations for, claims that a better vocabulary is available. Interesting philosophy is rarely an examination of the pros and cons of a thesis. Usually it is, implicitly or explicitly, a contest between an entrenched vocabulary which has become a nuisance and a half-formed new vocabulary which vaguely promises great things.

> (1989, 9)

Rorty, in short, is in the business of selling us a new outlook. He's inviting us to have a gestalt shift, to see things and describe them in quite a different way. There is really only one argument – *the whole picture*. And the best way to counter Rorty's image is by giving a different picture. The narrative explanation of the success of science that I presented in the first chapter offered a rival picture. Maybe there's really nothing more we can do than that.

3

LATOUR'S PROSAIC SCIENCE

The most embarrassing thing about 'facts' is the etymology of the word. The Latin *facere* means to make or construct. Bruno Latour, like so many other anti-realists who revel in the word's history, thinks facts are made by us: they are a social construction. The view acquires some plausibility in *Laboratory Life: The Social Construction of Scientific Facts* (hereafter *LL*) which Latour co-authored with Steve Woolgar (Latour and Woolgar 1979). This work, first published over a decade ago, has become a classic in the sociology of science literature.[1] It is in the form of field notes by an 'anthropologist in the lab'. This may seem an odd place for an anthropologist, but Latour finds his presence easy to justify: 'Whereas we have a fairly detailed knowledge of the myths and circumcision rituals of exotic tribes, we remain relatively ignorant of the details of equivalent activity among tribes of scientists . . .' (*LL*, 17).

LL has an amazing story to tell about the creation/discovery of TRF(H) (for thyrotropin releasing factor or hormone). The accepted view (whether created or discovered) is that this is a very rare substance produced by the hypothalamus which plays a major role in the endocrine system. TRF(H) triggers the release of the hormone thyrotropin by the pituitary gland; this hormone in turn governs the thyroid gland which controls growth, maturation and metabolism.

The work on TRF(H) was done by Andrew Schally and Roger Guillemin, independently; they shared the Nobel Prize in 1977 as co-discoverers, though each disputed the other's claim. The amount of physical labour involved in isolating TRF(H) is mind-boggling. Guillemin, for example, had 500 tons of pig's brains shipped to his lab in Texas; Schally worked with a comparable

41

amount of sheep's brains. Yet, the quantity of TRF(H) extracted in each case was tiny.

The lack of any significant amount of the hormone leads to an identification problem. As the existence of the stuff is somewhat precarious, any test for its presence is highly problematic. Latour's philosophical claims about facts largely turn on this. Consider gold: we have lots of this stuff; it is observable, easily recognized by ordinary people, paradigm samples abound. To protect ourselves from 'fool's gold' and from outright fraud, tests (assays) have been developed. How do we know that a particular assay is a good test? Simple. We use standard samples of gold and non-gold; an assay is a good one in so far as it can distinguish between them.

But such a procedure is not possible in the TRF(H) case. We simply do not have recognizable, independently given, samples that we can use to 'test the test'. Different bioassays for TRF(H) were developed by different research teams; but without a standard sample of TRF(H) there is no independent check on the bioassay; i.e. there is no way to be sure the bioassay is really 'true to the facts'. The relevant fact is this: there is a substance in the hypothalamus that releases the hormone thyrotropin from the pituitary and its chemical structure is pyroGlu-His-Pro-NH$_2$.

The *existence of the fact* rests on *acceptance of some particular bioassay*; they stand or fall together. At least this is what *LL* argues. The exact claim made by Latour and Woolgar is this: 'Without a bioassay a substance could not be said to exist' (*LL*, 64). There is no argument for this claim; apparently it is just obvious to all 'anthropologists in the lab'.[2] And it is also taken as obvious that since there is no *direct* test of the bioassay, it must have been adopted as a result of *social* negotiation. Schematically:

TRF(H) exists if and only if bioassay B is accepted
B is accepted as a result of social negotiation
∴ TRF(H) is not discovered; it is a social construction

The argument is interesting and the story behind it sufficiently engrossing that the conclusion is plausible. But after a bit of reflection we can see that neither premiss is acceptable. For example, the first means that there was no gold until there was an assay for it. There is, of course, a long tradition of theories of meaning and truth which link facts to tests (e.g.

verificationism). But a plausible version of such a theory must be able to distinguish the truth from what is tentatively believed to be the truth. (Usually this is done by talking of what is 'verifiable in the ideal limit'.) The link suggested in *LL* between fact and bioassay is much too crude to be in any way believable.

Perhaps this is an uncharitable reading of their words. As I mentioned above, the exact claim is: 'Without a bioassay a substance could not be said to exist.' This may just mean that without a test we have no grounds for *asserting* the existence of the stuff. Fine. This leaves it entirely open whether the stuff in question (gold, TRF(H)) actually exists. Consequently, facts needn't be social constructions after all, contrary to *LL*. This, of course, is the boring interpretation of events – but it is also the right one.

What about the second premiss of the argument? The picture painted by *LL* is reminiscent of Quine's 'web of belief'. Propositions are connected to one another in a network. Sometimes the connections are strong, at other times weak; but in any case the network is huge. Latour's picture is again initially plausible; much of our belief about any substance is intimately connected to whatever bioassays we have adopted. Sociologists of science are often acutely sensitive to this network feature of scientific beliefs and very skilled at making the multitude of complexities in our web of belief manifest. (Philosophers, by contrast, often tell impoverished fairy-tales to illustrate their theses.) But when it comes to drawing morals many sociologists of science become suddenly and strangely simplistic. Latour's network, for instance, consists of only the two propositions: 'This is TRF(H)' and 'This is the bioassay that works'. They are linked in such a way that they stand or fall together.

Such simplemindedness is easily countered. In the bioassay which has been adopted rats are used instead of mice because mice are believed to have more sensitive thyroids; males are used instead of females because the female reproductive cycle might interfere; 80-day-old rats are used since that is the age when the thyrotropin content of the pituitary is greatest; etc. Of course, these are fallible considerations often loaded with unwarranted assuptions (e.g. why take females at certain stages of their reproductive cycle as abnormal?); but the crucial thing is that they are *independent* reasons for thinking that the particular bioassay adopted is the right one for detecting TRF(H). Ian Hacking (whom I rely on here) discusses the complications of TRF(H) bioassays. He takes the number of variables involved to be 'staggering' (1988, 283) and to be reason for initial (but not ultimate) sympathy with Latour and Woolgar. I prefer to see this mass of complications as a multitude of connections into our overall network. *Contra* Latour, we do not have a little circle consisting of only two propositions[3] which will stand or fall together – we have a very much larger network and the bioassay is supported by numerous far-reaching strands.

It may be a social construction that rats have more sensitive thyroids than mice, but it was not constructed by the TRF(H) gang. For them, it functions as a kind of external constraint. So, the claim that the bioassay is accepted through social negotiation will be much harder to sustain. Once we allow that people have to work (even when they have an eye on their own interests) with facts which are *not constructed by them*, we might as well admit the possibility that sometimes people have to work with facts which are *not constructed, simpliciter*.

The theme of the social creation of facts runs through all of Latour's works. The more recent *Science in Action: How to Follow Scientists and Engineers Through Society* (1987) (hereafter *SA*) adds a temporal element to the creation of facts. 'By itself *a given sentence is neither a fact nor a fiction; it is made so by others, later on*' (*SA*, 25). This bold pronouncement acquires the dignified position of being the '*First Principle*: The fate of facts and machines is in the later users' hands; their qualities are thus a consequence, not a cause, of the collective action' (*SA*, 258). It would seem the actions and antics of historical actors matter much less than their audience. The latter-day spectator endows the earlier action with significance. One would like to know how long before this significance takes effect; how long before a fact becomes a fact. A few minutes? A few years? Copernicus's utterances were neither true nor false in the sixteenth century, it would seem; but Newton and others in the seventeenth century made them true. Was that the end of the matter? Or did Einstein and the rest of us in the twentieth century make them false? The same could be said of Newton and Einstein themselves. But what remarkable power is it that Newton had in half-measure, that he could make the statements of Copernicus true, yet he could not make his own statements true?

Latour's argument for no-truth-value-until-later is simply to cite the phenomenon of *shifting belief* – which is not enough to justify the deep ontological claims about facts which are here asserted. That people change their minds *does not tell* against facts. Though unaware, Latour is simply (though often interestingly and skilfully) describing what any philosopher would call a coherence theory of justification. It should not be confused with a social theory of truth. Latour would be more believable – but less original – if he said later scientists made the theories of earlier ones stick. It was Newton who made Kepler believable; it was Euler who made Newton stick.

The great weakness of this work is in the systematic failure to appreciate the subtleties of arguments in support of a theory. For example, there are some rather naive remarks about the argument from authority. Latour notes that philosophers and scientists dismiss such appeals; but he thinks that as a matter of fact such appeals are common and effective. Footnoting, for example, is viewed as a rhetorical device.

> The effect of references on persuasion is not limited to that of 'prestige' or 'bluff'. Again, it is a question of *numbers*. A paper that does not have references is like a child without an escort walking at night in a big city it does not know: isolated, lost, anything may happen to it. On the contrary, attacking a paper heavy with footnotes means that the dissenter has to weaken each of the other papers, or will at least be threatened with having to do so, whereas attacking a naked paper means that the reader and the author are of the same weight: face to face.
>
> (*SA*, 33)

This is an absurdly cynical view of what most of us would ordinarily consider the marshalling of evidence. It is also strikingly at odds with some interesting empirical results which point in a sociological direction all right, but in a direction opposite to Latour's. This is the very well-known phenomenon that physics articles typically have many fewer references than articles in the social sciences – the reverse of their normally perceived order of authority.

There is yet a more important point. References by themselves mean nothing. If, in the present chapter, I were to include 150 footnotes to the work of Einstein, it would mean nothing.

The appeals to authority must be appropriately integrated; I must show that my conclusions are appropriately connected to the work of the authors who are being cited; for example, there might be a derivation of a new conclusion using the earlier work as a premiss.

Latour, however, will have none of this. In *The Pasteurization of France* (1988) (hereafter *PF*) he declares 'There has never been such a thing as deduction' (*PF*, 176). He goes on to explain:

> 'Reason' is applied to the work of allocating agreement and disagreement between words. It is a matter of taste and feeling, know-how and connoisseurship, class and status. We insult, pout, clench our fists, enthuse, spit, sigh, and dream. Who reasons?
>
> (*PF*, 179f.)

Who indeed?

In the first half of *PF* Latour interestingly traces the influence of Pasteur (and the initial small handful of Pasteurians) on the hygienists. The latter constituted a large group interested in cleaning things up, in reversing the physical and moral degeneration of the general population, especially the poor. The hygienists had no particular views about the causes and nature of disease, though they were not in the least impressed with 'contagion' theories advanced before Pasteur.

What Latour is mainly interested in doing is uncovering how accomplishments such as this large 'social movement for regeneration' came to be seen as the achievements of a single man – Pasteur.

> Where would the hygienist movement have gone without Pasteur and his followers? In its own direction. Without the microbe, without vaccine, even without the doctrine of contagion or the variation in virulence, everything that was done could have been done: cleaning up the towns; digging drains; demanding running water, light, air and heat. . . . The fulcrum provided by bacteriology should not let us forget that the enormous social movement was working for that mixture of urbanism, consumer protection, ecology (as we would say nowadays), defense of the environment, and moralization summed up by the word *hygiene*.
>
> (*PF*, 23)

The issue must to some extent remain unsettled, since the relation in general between medicine and hygiene in improving human well-being remains a contentious matter. Latour's central claim is that '[Pasteur's discoveries] were convincing because the hygienists believed them and forced everybody else *to put them into practice*' (*PF*, 54). Of course, this brings us back to the question of facts. Did microbes exist *before* Pasteur? Did he discover them? Are they real?

> In the laboratory any new object is at first defined by inscribing in the laboratory notebook a long list of what the agent does and does not do. This definition of the agent is acceptable, but it runs the risk of bringing us a new philosophical problem. Did the microbe exist before Pasteur? From the practical point of view – I say practical, not theoretical – it did not.
>
> (*PF*, 80)

So microbes aren't real – not in the practical sense (whatever that means – Latour doesn't say). But are they real in some other sense? Latour's answer is mostly no; but it's far from unequivocal.

> Once the statistical apparatus that reveals the danger of anthrax and the efficacy of the vaccine, has been stabilized, . . . once Pasteur has linked his bacillus with each movement made by the 'anthrax', then and only then is the double impression made: the microbe has been discovered and the vaccine is distributed everywhere. . . . I would be prepared to say that Pasteur had 'really discovered' the truth of the microbe at last, if the word 'true' would add more than confusion.
>
> (*PF*, 93)

One of the more remarkable features of Latour's work is the centrality of the text, of words, and in general, of inscriptions. The theme first arose in *LL*, and the hermeneutical influence continues unabated in the two later books, *SA* and *PF*. Instead of texts being the way we record data and communicate our thoughts and theories, texts themselves hold centre stage in the scientific process.

> Behind the texts [scientists] have mobilized inscriptions [i.e. more texts], and huge and costly instruments to obtain

these inscriptions. But something else resists the trials of strength behind the instruments, something that I will call provisionally a new object.

(*SA*, 87)

Does this reference to 'object' mean that Latour recognizes that all these texts might be *about* something which is not just more text? Might it be about the world? Alas, no.

What counts for us is to understand the new object just at the moment of its emergence. Inside the laboratory the new object is *a list of written answers to trials*.

(*SA*, 87)

And in the same vein,

We do not think. We do not have ideas. Rather there is the action of *writing*, an action which involves working with *inscriptions* that have been extracted; an action that is practised through *talking* to other people who likewise write, inscribe, talk, and live in similarly unusual places; an action that *convinces* or fails to convince with inscriptions which are made to speak, to write, and to be read.

(*PF*, 218)

Ordinary anthropologists distinguish the natives' doings from the natives' reports of their doings. The latter is useful evidence in theorizing about the former; but it is certainly not to be taken at face value. Latour similarly refuses to take science at face value.

We take the apparent superiority of the members of our laboratory in technical matters to be insignificant. . . . This is similar to the anthropologist's refusal to bow before the knowledge of the primitive sorcerer. . . . There are . . . no a priori reasons for supposing that the scientist's practice is any more rational than that of outsiders.

(*LL*, 29f)

If we ask scientists what they are doing, we get answers such as: 'Determining the magnetic moment of the electron', 'Setting up a device to detect solar neutrinos', 'Trying to renormalize my quantum theory of gravitation', 'Determining the effects of TRF(H) on the metabolism of rats' etc. In general they might be prepared to say that they are trying to figure out how the world works. Is this the picture that the anthropologist in the lab *finally* adopts, after initial agnosticism? Not in the least. Latour sees scientists as having 'developed considerable skills in setting up devices which can pin down elusive figures, traces, or inscriptions in their craftwork, and in the art of persuasion. . . . They are so skillful', he continues, 'that they manage to convince others not that they are being convinced but that they are simply following a consistent line of interpretation of the available evidence' (*LL*, 69f.).

The aim of any working scientist is not to uncover the facts but to produce texts. Words, charts, diagrams, plots and other inscriptions are the principal output of any laboratory. Inscriptions do not record or reflect the data; in some sense they are the data, the raw material to be worked on. This prosaic analysis of science gives new meaning to 'publish or perish'. Of course, our anthropologist's caution is entirely correct in not taking the scientists' self-description at face value; any other attitude would simply beg the question. But we may err in the other direction. While we needn't a priori take their pronouncements at face value, scientist's self-descriptions may nevertheless be correct, and we should allow the possibility of discovering that this is so. Latour, in the field, writes of himself:

The anthropologist feels vindicated in having retained his anthropological perspective in the face of the beguiling charms of his informants: they claim merely to be scientists discovering facts; he doggedly argued that they were writers and readers in the business of being convinced and convincing others. Initially this seemed a moot or even absurd standpoint, but now it appeared far more reasonable. The problem for participants was to persuade readers of papers (and constituent diagrams and figures) that its statements should be accepted as fact. To this end rats had been bled and beheaded, frogs had been flayed, chemicals consumed, time spent, careers had been made and broken, and inscription devices had been manufactured and accumulated within the laboratory. By remaining steadfastly obstinate, our anthropologist observer resisted the temptation to be convinced by the facts. Instead, he was able to portray laboratory activity as the organization of persuasion through literary inscription.

(*LL*, 88)

Such steadfast obstinateness can only be greeted with awe; and such powers of resistance are only to be marvelled at.

The persuasive element of the scientific process has nothing to do with 'evidence' or 'reason'; it is, according to Latour, largely political. The negotiations that scientists enter into to create alliances etc. he calls 'Machiavellian' (*SA*, 125):

> The general strategy is easy to grasp: do what you need to the former literature to render it as helpful as possible for the claims you are going to make. The rules are simple enough: weaken your enemies, paralyse those you cannot weaken . . . , help your allies if they are attacked, ensure safe communications with those who supply you with indisputable instruments . . . , oblige your enemies to fight one another . . . ; if you are not sure of winning, be humble and understated. These are simple rules indeed: the rules of the oldest politics.

(*SA*, 38)

Facts get to be facts when groups with overlapping interests support one another.

> [Franz] Boas, the American anthropologist, is engaged in a fierce controversy against eugenicists. . . . Suppose, now, that a young anthropologist demonstrates that, at least in one Samoan island, biology cannot be the cause of crisis in adolescent girls because cultural determinism is too strong. Is not Boas going to be 'interested' in [Margaret] Mead's report . . . ? Every time eugenicists criticise his cultural determinism, Boas will fasten his threatened position to Mead's counter-example. But every time Boas and other anthropologists do so, they turn Mead's story more into a fact.

(*SA*, 109)

Finding a social motive to account for a scientific move is standard fare for sociologists of science. There is a rather intriguing account of this in *LL*. 'What drives scientists', ask Latour and Woolgar, 'to set up inscription devices, write papers, construct objects, and occupy different positions?' (*LL*, 189). The answer seems entirely reasonable: they want the recognition of their peers; they want credit for the work they do. Latour and Woolgar go on to make much of this notion of 'credit'.

> It would be wrong to regard the receipt of reward as the ultimate objective of scientific activity. In fact, the receipt of reward is just one small portion of a large cycle of credibility investment. The essential feature of this cycle is the gain of credibility which enables reinvestment and the further gain of credibility. Consequently, there is no ultimate objective to scientific investment other than the continual redeployment of accumulated resources. It is in this sense we liken scientists' credibility to a cycle of capital investment.
>
> (LL, 198)

The analogy is an interesting one. There is a striking similarity between capital re-investment and the growth of a scientist's credibility. But the similarity is overblown. Not all capital, after all, is re-invested; some is pocketed to buy the necessities of life and many a pleasure, too. But that is not really the point. Do capitalists only make money? Successful ones seem to make a lot of money, but they make more besides. They make artifacts. And don't they make money because they make artifacts? Of course, many manufactured items are silly and useless; they are sold through deceptive advertising, not because of their intrinsic worth. Nevertheless, other goods, like my personal computer, live up to their promise. Because of this, someone made some money from me. Without for a moment conceding the justice or efficacy of capitalism as a social institution, it remains an obvious truth that some capitalists make money because they produce useful products. If we adopt the analogy of Latour and Woolgar, how can we resist saying that some scientists – though certainly not all – get credit because they produce good theories?

There are times when Latour turns his back on any *interest* account of science – at least if those interests have anything to do with society. His principal reason for opposing interest explanations is that the sciences will sometimes 'revolutionize the very conception of society' (PF, 38).

> Right from the first pages of this book [i.e. SA] the reader may have noticed the shocking absence of the entities that traditionally make up Society, an absence that may be even

more shocking than the delayed appearance of Nature . . .
there has been not a word yet on social classes, on capitalism, . . . not a single discussion of culture. . . . I suggest
that we follow scientists and engineers at work and it turns
out that *they do not know what society is made of*, any more
than they know the nature of Nature beforehand. It is
because they know about neither that they are so busy
trying out new associations, creating an inside world in
which to work, displacing interests, negotiating facts, re-
shuffling groups and recruiting new allies.

(*SA*, 142)

Not even the most die-hard rationalist (me, for example) would
deny that much science has been motivated by social interests.[4]
Latour's motivation for this remark is his belief that society is the
result of settling a dispute, not the cause of it. But this just seems
a simple confusion. Surely the right thing for Latour to say is
that *earlier society* plays a role in the formation of results and
disputes, and those in turn play a role in the construction of *later
society*.[5]

Nevertheless, there is something insightful about his point.
Latour is uneasy about David Bloor's (1976/1991) 'strong programme'. What he wants to do is to embrace the so-called
'symmetry principle' and to generalize it some way or other.[6]
This might make for an improvement. As it stands, the strong
programme makes science out to be just so much epiphen-
omena hovering over the real world of social life. At least in
Latour's hands, society (initially) does not receive such a privi-
leged position.

Yet, at other times, mundane interest explanations seem
exactly what he has in mind as the thing which fuels the engine
of science.

Either the physicians could use what was taking place in
the Institut Pasteur to advance their own interests, or they
could not. If they could, any argument, *however revolutionary it might be*, would be understood, seized upon, trans-
ported, and used as soon as possible. . . . But if they could
not, no argument, *however useful and important it might be* in
the eyes of others, could be understood or applied even
after a century.

(*PF*, 120)

In spite of the promise of a new and improved analysis of science, we find the same old pattern of explanation – people believe what they believe because of social factors. In spite of the intriguing assertion early in *PF* that rationalist and sociological approaches are alike dismissed (*PF*, 6), and the bold pronouncement near the end that 'Nothing is, by itself, either reducible or irreducible to anything else' (*PF*, 158), we find that when push comes to shove it is the tired old social interest that makes the scientific world go around.

Why do so many would-be sociologists of science find *rational explanations* implausible? Sociologists of science from Barnes and Bloor to Collins and Latour seem to find 'reason', 'evidence' and similar notions highly problematic. Seldom do they spell out their objections explicitly, but I strongly suspect that they find these sorts of notions unbelievable in principle. Like the tooth fairy, 'evidence' is something that only philosophers and children believe in. For example, Latour calls his own account the 'translation' model of science; he contrasts it with the 'diffusion' model (*SA*, 133, 134). What he says about the latter is revealing.

> If, to explain the 'diffusion' of Pasteur's ideas, we had nothing more than the force of Pasteur and his collaborators, those ideas would never have left the walls of the Ecole Normal laboratory and would not have even *entered* them. An idea, even an idea of genius, even an idea that is to save millions of people, never moves of its own accord. It requires a force to fetch it, seize upon it for its own motives, move it, and often transform it.
>
> (*PF*, 16)

The causal abilities of reason are ridiculed.

> When we talk of 'thought', even the most sceptical lose their faculties. Like vulgar sorcerers, they let 'thought' travel like magic at high speed over great distances. I do not know anyone who is not credulous when it comes to ideas.
>
> (*PF*, 218)

The spirit behind these remarks is the firm belief that an idea, a reason, a piece of evidence is not the sort of stuff that could make things happen. They are like shadows – caused by the real stuff of the world, but incapable of doing anything in their own right. In particular, no idea of Pasteur's could mobilize millions of people; only a social force could do that.

What all of this betrays, I suspect, is a confusion about reasons and causes. The topic has a long and involved history, and I won't review it here. I can do no more than dogmatically pronounce: *reasons are causes.*[7] The rationalist account of the scientific process is not in the least acausal; it simply appeals to a rather special type of cause: reason. Once this is admitted, much of the wind is taken out of the sociologists' sails.

Though I have been brief on the business of reasons and causes, the issue is no small matter in the sociology of science literature. I suspect that the implicit denial that reasons are causes is linked to what can only be called a behaviourist methodology. Thinking, intending, reasoning and similar mental processes are downplayed or even dismissed in the investigation of science. Overt actions and words as physical inscriptions are the only sorts of things which figure in the laboratory anthropologist's data. Such an impoverished methodology has led to a hopeless account of human psychology. By the same token, such an impoverished methodology for understanding the lab leads to a similarly hopeless account of the workings of science.

Many of Latour's arguments are ill-conceived and misdirected. If his conclusions were to be believed, it would have the effect of undermining the authority of science. One can't help wondering if this is indeed his aim. Latour finally steps out of his role as anthropologist of the lab (the neutral observer) and remarks on what he sees as the larger significance of science, especially contemporary science, as revealed by his own work. He assails fraudulent reason.

It is at this point that the paths of revealers of microbes and the path of people like me part. We no longer have to fight against microbes, but against the misfortunes of reason – and that, too, makes us weep. This is why we need other proofs, other actors, other paths, and is why we challenge those scientists. Because we have other interests and follow other ways, we find the myth of reason and science unacceptable, intolerable, even immoral. We are no longer, alas, at the end of the nineteenth century, the most beautiful of centuries, but at the end of the twentieth, and

a major source of pathology and mortality is reason itself –
its works, its pomps, and its armaments.

(*PF*, 149)

Of course, two can play the game of moral outrage. A few years
ago smallpox was completely eradicated from the earth. A
joyous occasion – yet Latour finds science 'unacceptable'. A
short while ago the gene for cystic fibrosis was located. This will
help to alleviate untold misery for children and their parents –
yet Latour finds science 'intolerable'. Work at a feverish rate is
being done to find a cure or a vaccine for AIDS. With success the
lives of millions will be saved – yet Latour finds science
'immoral'. 'My account', says Latour, 'will seem convincing
only if it allows readers to go faster in the direction that they
wanted to go in any case' (*PF*, 148). A frank admission. But there
is no need to join such readers on the road to hell. There is a
better way to see science.

Perhaps Latour doesn't mean what he says. He may, with
very good reason, have particular chunks of science in mind
which rightly deserve condemnation. On far too many oc-
casions science has been used for pernicious social ends, and
one might come to see science itself as the enemy, as something
'unacceptable, intolerable, even immoral'. On the other hand,
Latour is naive in thinking that this is a feature of twentieth
century science. The nineteenth century ('the most beautiful
of centuries') is replete with monstrous examples: doctrines of
hysteria, of race and intelligence, craniometry and Social
Darwinism, to name but a few.

However, Scientific Ludditism is the last thing we want. What
we need is an analysis of science that can be selectively critical –
total damnation is as pernicious as complete idolatry and as silly
as scientism. For the sake of a contrast with Latour, I'll turn to a
recent feminist critic of science, and we shall see that even a
relatively conservative methodology of science can be turned
into a powerful critical tool when directed at particular pieces of
science.

Helen Longino's *Science as Social Knowledge* (hereafter *SSK*) has
the aim of reconciling 'the objectivity of science with its social
and cultural construction' (*SSK*, ix). While allowing that science
is replete with values, she distinguishes between the 'auton-
omy' and the 'integrity' of science. Of course, science is not

autonomous; there are external social forces at work on science all the time. But Longino wishes to deny the other sense of value-free science, too. She thinks 'contextual values' influence observation, inference, theory construction etc. just as outside forces direct many of the aims of science. It is important to know which of these types of values is doing what when.

Her view combines two main ingredients. One of these has to do with objectivity:

> There are standards of rational acceptability that are independent of particular interests and values but the satisfaction of these standards by a theory or hypothesis does not guarantee that the theory or hypothesis in question is value- or interest-free.
>
> (SSK, 12)

I shall not pursue the details of Longino's specific methodological proposals. Suffice it to say that they involve many of the standard ingredients, such as: that data can be specified independently of any theory; that there is a logical gap between data and theory; and consequently, that data (fallibly) support a theory only in the context of some set of background assumptions.

The fact that there is such a gap and that background assumptions are needed in the process of scientific inference leads to Longino's other main ingredient in standard methodology. This is the desirability of constantly probing into the value-ladenness of these background beliefs; but more importantly, it includes the desirability of producing rival theories which utilize different (value-laden) background beliefs. Values are visible only by contrast. 'Until such alternatives are available,' says Longino, 'community assumptions are transparent [i.e. invisible] to their adherents' (SSK, 80).

> The greater the number of different points of view included in a given community, the more likely it is that its scientific practice will be objective, that is, that it will result in descriptions and explanations of natural processes that are more reliable in the sense of less characterized by idiosyncratic subjective preferences of community members than would otherwise be the case.
>
> (SSK, 80)

By contextualizing evidence, Longino allows us to interpret

the actions of rival scientists as equally rational. 'Once it is accepted that the evidential relation is always determined by background assumptions, it is easy to see', says Longino, 'that there could be a neutral description of a given state of affairs, and no agreement on the hypotheses for which it is taken as evidence. It is also easy to see that both parties are being rational' (*SSK*, 60).

The relativization of evidence raises a potential problem. Does it lead to the complete relativization of knowledge? Longino thinks not.

> As long as background beliefs can be articulated and sub-jected to criticism from the scientific community, they can be defended, modified, or abandoned in response to such criticism. As long as this kind of response is possible, the incorporation of hypotheses into the canon of scientific knowledge can be independent of any individual's subjec-tive preferences.
>
> (*SSK*, 74)

These considerations can be brought to bear on specific examples such as theorizing about human evolution, which Longino discusses in considerable detail. (I rely on her account in what follows.) The search for human origins – both anatom-ical and social – has enormous social ramifications. It informs our picture of ourselves, and so plays a role in the determination of social policy and civil life.

One prominent hypothesis is the 'man-the-hunter' view. The development of tools, on this account, is a direct result of hunting by males. When tools are used for killing animals and for threatening or even killing other humans, the canine tooth (which had played a major role in aggressive behaviour) loses its importance, and so there will be evolutionary pressure favour-ing more effective molar functioning, for example. Thus human morphology is linked to male behaviour. Male aggression, in the form of hunting behaviour, is linked to intelligence, in the form of tool making. Notice that in this account women play no role in evolution. We are what we are today because of our male ancestors' activities.

But this is not the only view of our origin. A theory of more recent vintage is the 'woman-the-gatherer' hypothesis. This account sees the development of tool use to be a function of female behaviour. As humans moved from the plentiful forests to the less abundant grasslands, the need for gathering food over a wide territory increased. Moreover, women are always under greater stress than men since they need to feed both themselves and their young. Thus, there was greater selective pressure on females to be inventive. And so, innovations with tools were due mainly to females. Why, on this account, should males lose their large canine teeth? The answer is sexual selection. Females preferred males who were more sociable, less prone to bare their fangs and to other displays of aggression.

So, on the 'woman-the-gatherer' account of our origins, our anatomical and social evolution is based on women's activities. On this account we are what we are today largely because of the endeavours of our female ancestors.

The kinds of evidential consideration thought relevant in deciding this issue include: fossils, objects identified as tools, the behaviour of contemporary primates and the activities of contemporary gatherer–hunter peoples. Obviously, each of these is somewhat problematic. Fossils, for example, are few and far between, and are little more than fragments; some tools such as sticks will not last the way stone tools will, so we may have a very misleading sample of primitive artifacts; moreover, it is often debatable whether any alleged tool was really used for hunting an animal or preparing it for eating, rather than for preparing some vegetation for consumption; and finally, inferences from the behaviour of contemporary primates and gatherer–hunter humans to the nature of our ancestors who lived 2–12 million years ago is a leap that only a Kierkegaard would relish.

None of these considerations should be dismissed out of hand; each provides evidence of some sort, but it is painfully weak. We have a case of radical underdetermination – there simply is not enough evidence to pick out a winner from these two rival theories. Nevertheless, our ability or inability to find the right theory is not important. The moral of this example is that it displays how values can affect choices. If one is already inclined to think of males as the inventors of tools, then some chipped stone will be interpreted as, say, a tool for hunting. This will then become powerful evidence in the man-the-hunter account of our origin. On the other hand, if one is a feminist then one might be inclined to see some alleged tool as an implement for the preparation of vegetable foods. On this interpretation the tool becomes strong evidence for the woman-the-gatherer account of our evolution.

We may hope, with Longino, that 'In time, a less gender-centric account of human evolution may eventually supersede both of these current contending stories' (SSK, 111). It will not, however, be a value-free view of the matter. Values will always play a role in any scientific theorizing; it is just a matter of getting clear on this and making the operative values visible. The great merit of the woman-the-gatherer theory is that its very existence made manifest the androcentrism of the prior man-the-hunter theory. Until the existence of the rival, the 'evidence' for the man-the-hunter account was 'dependent upon culturally embedded sexist assumptions' (SSK, 111).

There need be nothing wrong in principle with the presence of values in science; after all they might be the 'right' values, and even if not, the theory could be right anyway. What is wrong is thinking that facts dictate theories all by themselves – they get lots of help. And we make scientific progress when we reveal the character of that help.

As critics of science, there are many differences between Latour and Longino, but the most significant of these turns on the extent – not the severity – of any piece of criticism. '[C]ounterideologies, if they are to be useful in changing science,' says Longino, 'must be brought to bear locally on specific research programs' (SSK, 187). Latour, on the other hand, tars with a brush so wide there is nothing left worth seeing. Longino offers us the hope of an improved science; Latour offers us only cynical nihilism.

4

THE NATURALISM OF RUSE

NATURALISM AND EVOLUTION

Naturalism is the currently fashionable view that somehow or other norms can be eliminated in favour of facts about a purely physical world. According to Michael Ruse's *Taking Darwin Seriously: A Naturalistic Approach to Philosophy* (1986) (hereafter *TDS*), the norms of epistemology and ethics are to be accounted for by the theory of evolution; our dispositions to think and act in the ways we do are the result of a natural Darwinian process. Naturalism of any sort seems highly attractive, since it eliminates these somewhat mysterious entities (norms), and who, after all, wants to be *un*natural? (There is something in a name, isn't there?)

But just what is naturalism? It seems a rather vague notion allowing lots of latitude (which further accounts for much of its appeal), yet characterizing it along the following lines does not seem too off track. Consider the following two questions.

1 How *do* we acquire beliefs, attitudes and practices?
2 How *ought* we to acquire beliefs, attitudes and practices?

Naturalists are those who think that only question (1) matters; or that (2) is a hopeless question since there is no such thing as a normative standard with which to judge; or that an answer to (1) will be, in fact, an answer to (2); or that we cannot answer (2) until we know the answer to (1). Naturalism in most of its guises is a reductionistic programme. Physical objects, properties and processes are taken to be the basic stuff of reality. Norms, whether epistemic or ethical, are eliminated, explained away, or somehow accounted for in terms of the physical. Michael Ruse is definitely in the naturalist mould, and his account of knowledge and ethics is one of the more promising versions in that tradition.

Ruse is a major Darwin scholar who has contributed a vast amount to the history and philosophy of biology. His *TDS* uses the theory of evolution to explain (or explain away) much of our cognitive life. It starts with a clear presentation of the basics of Darwin's theory of evolution, and it might be worthwhile reviewing some of these. The theory asserts three things. First, there is *variation*; different members of a species have different characteristics. Second, there is *differential* selection; individuals with some types of characteristics are more likely to survive than others with different characteristics (i.e. 'survival of the fittest'). Third, there is *inheritance* or *retention*; offspring tend to resemble their parents more closely than they resemble non-relations. From these three factors the *evolution* of species follows. Though simple, the theory is easily misunderstood. Notions of progress and improvement are the common pitfalls. Species are not getting 'better', and evolutionary progress is not 'toward' anything. Evolutionary change is just adaptation, not improvement.

EPISTEMOLOGY

Broadly, there are two quite distinct approaches which go under the name 'evolutionary epistemology'. One of these sees the development of science as importantly similar to the evolution of biological species. The other view does not concern itself with theory *change*, but instead focuses on our nature as knowers. It is concerned with human cognitive capacity as a product of the evolutionary process; it holds that we are 'hardwired' to think in a rather specific manner. To keep these separate, Ruse labels the first 'evolutionary epistemology' and the second 'Darwinian epistemology'. (I shall stick to his useful labels, though readers should note that this terminology is not standard.)

Ruse's discussion of the scientific change/biological evolution analogy (i.e. what he calls evolutionary epistemology) is clear, critical and persuasive. The analogy, in a nut shell, says that scientific theories change in the same way that biological species evolve. Theories are born into a jungle red in tooth and claw;

they fight to survive and they eventually die, though often they pass on many of their characteristics to subsequent theories.

This analogy between the growth of science and the evolution of species can be viewed in at least two ways. In the hands of Herbert Spencer or Karl Popper, the analogy plays the role of shedding light on the nature of knowledge. Given that we understand how organisms evolve, we can now better grasp the nature of developing science. On the other hand, Stephen Toulmin's (1972) use of the evolutionary analogy is much stronger. He thinks the growth of science is not merely similar to what goes on in the biological world; he thinks the processes are identical. Belief is actually governed by the laws of evolution. Toulmin's is arguably a more significant claim since it clearly dissolves the normative question. On Popper's view we can still raise the normative issue, 'Yes, this is the way knowledge develops, but ought it to do so? Perhaps we could do better.' But if Toulmin is right, then there simply is no point in asking whether this is the way things should happen. Just as the laws of nature simply *are* and we do not ask 'Ought force to equal mass times acceleration?', so there is no point in asking if we ought to believe what in fact we do believe. (Perhaps God as creator of those laws has something to answer for, but not us.) The development of belief is governed by a law of nature, and the law is Darwin's.

Is evolutionary epistemology in any of its variants correct? Ruse thinks not, and he is absolutely right. There are several reasons for rejecting the analogy.[1] We do not get random variation in new conjectures; theories are highly directed. Unlike the mechanistic nature of evolutionary processes in the physical world, a teleological account is needed to do justice to scientific theorizing. Moreover (though this is not mentioned by Ruse), the flourishing of astrological and other such silly beliefs must be a great embarrassment to any evolutionary epistemologist. In the struggle for survival astrology has proven to be very fit indeed, making it all the way into the US White House.[2]

A distinction can be made between theories and methods. The development of the latter has been slower and arguably not as directed as the former. Some (e.g. Rescher 1977) have argued for an evolutionary account of scientific *method*, while admitting that the evolutionary case for *theories* is hopeless. Ruse does not specifically take up this issue, but the view could easily be incorporated into his general discussion and dismissed for reasons similar to those given for rejecting ordinary evolutionary epistemology; so I shall not pursue the matter here.[3]

Ruse's positive view on the nature of human knowledge goes by the name 'Darwinian epistemology'. The central idea is that there are various human cognitive capacities which are hard-wired ways of thinking. They are the result of the evolutionary process; we think in the quite specific ways we do because they have survival value. This view is to be sharply contrasted with evolutionary epistemology where theories (or methods) are seen as evolving in the same way as species. Darwinian epistemology, in general, says instead that we are hard-wired to believe certain things or to proceed methodologically in certain narrowly circumscribed ways.

Ruse's version of Darwinian epistemology focuses on scientific practice and inference patterns, as opposed to the specific content of theories or beliefs. He does not, for instance, suggest that we are genetically determined to believe that $F = ma$ or that grass is green; instead he thinks we are programmed to reason in definite ways. Thus, for the most part, it is the methodological procedure and not the theoretical content which is genetically fixed; it is the way of thinking, not the result, which is biologically conditioned.

> [T]he methods of science are rooted in selective necessity, but . . . the product soars up gloriously into the highest reaches of culture, quite transcending its organic origins. And it is the epigenetic rules which play the key mediating role. The nature and development of science is constrained and informed by the biologically channelled modes of thinking imposed on us by evolution – a consequence of the reproductive struggle faced by humans. . . .
>
> (*TDS*, 149)

Nature has not given us quantum mechanics or relativity or any other scientific theory. Instead it has given us the tools to come up with them ourselves. These tools are the usual sort of inductive and deductive rules of inference.

> [T]he methodology . . . leading to [present] science . . . is produced by Darwinian-selected epigenetic rules. There

are rules for approval of *modus ponens* and consiliences, no less than there is a rule setting up incest barriers.

(*TDS*, 160f.)

'Epigenetic rules' are genetic-based regularities which channel the development of behavioural or cognitive traits. Ruse brings the notion over from sociobiology where they are posited to explain behaviour. His Darwinian epistemology (and his Darwinian ethics) are a rather natural extension of sociobiology into the cognitive realm. (So readers not enamoured with socio-biology will probably balk at Ruse's Darwinian epistemology and ethics as well.) The style of argument Ruse uses is the same as he and others use in drawing sociobiological conclusions:

Activity A has survival value
Characteristics which have survival value are genetically based
∴ Activity A is genetically based

For the sociobiologist, instances of A are reciprocal altruism, male aggression, female passivity, male philandering, homo-sexuality etc. For the Darwinian epistemologist, instances of activity A are deductive reasoning patterns in the style of *modus ponens*, and inferences based on inductive consiliences. The objections one can raise in principle against such a style of argument are already laid out in the vast literature critical of sociobiology.

It may well be that there is greater survival value in having less rather than more structure to our thinking. A plastic, and hence rather flexible, thought process may have been the prod-uct of natural selection. To think that adaptive behaviours must be innate just begs the question against this alternative outlook which is just as Darwinian in spirit. This, it seems to me, is the serious rival to Ruse's view. We should instead maintain that the evolutionary process has resulted in our having the capacity to think – but there are no biological constraints on what or how we think.

E. O. Wilson thinks 'genes have given away much of their sovereignty'. He allows an increasing role for culture, but he insists that 'genes hold culture on a leash' (cited in *TDS*, 143). Perhaps Ruse would like to maintain the same outlook – genes hold our scientific (and ethical) beliefs on a leash. The debate may become one about degrees: how long is the leash? Most people are probably willing to acknowledge some biological constraints on human theorizing, though I am inclined to believe there are none at all – but more of this later.

Ruse gives only a brief sketch of how he thinks science works. *Modus ponens* and consiliences of induction are central. Whether he is right or wrong in detail is of secondary importance. His primary thesis is that the basic structure of scientific reasoning (whatever standard scientific reasoning might be) is genetically based. There is lots of room for disagreement about the details. In this regard, as in so many others, the situation is analogous to sociobiology. For example, there are rival accounts of homosexuality. All sociobiologists see the existence of non-reproducing care-givers as adaptive, but they see this as coming about in different ways. One says it is the direct result of genetic make-up; another says that mothers are genetically programmed to psychologically manipulate one of their children into becoming a homosexual. Either way the result betters the survival chances of the grandchildren.

Consiliences of induction have been the subject of much philosophical controversy; but if they are not a part of good scientific practice, the worst outcome for Ruse is that he would have to change examples. Nevertheless, the reader could wish for more detail. Merely citing *modus ponens* and consiliences of induction is not much to go on. Does Ruse want to include all the standard (elementary) rules of deductive and inductive inference? If the answer is yes, then why do people so often commit the fallacies of affirming the consequent and denying the antecedent? On the other hand, if the answer is no, then what is the status of the non-genetically determined rules we regularly employ? If Ruse does not have a naturalistic account of these, then why have a naturalistic account of a limited few when a platonistic account could do the whole job?

One of the least contentious examples of an epigenetic rule at work is the way we classify colours. The spectrum is continuous, but humans see distinct colour intervals in it – red, yellow, blue etc. This classification is common to all cultures, which suggests that it is innate rather than any kind of learned convention (*TDS*, 143).

I find this example highly convincing; it strongly suggests that colour classification is indeed genetically determined. But notice that it also is a very bad example for the Darwinian epistemologist. We are convinced that the classification is innate largely because we think the classification scheme is *false*. Classification of the spectrum into distinct intervals may be adaptive (undoubtedly it is), but it is *not* the truth, and it is most especially *not* the way we must think about colours. We have learned to think about the spectrum as continuous, regardless of what we see.

In one place Ruse cites Quine approvingly:

> Why should our subjective spacing of qualities have a special purchase on nature . . . ?
>
> There is some encouragement in Darwin. If people's innate spacing of qualities is a gene-linked trait, then the spacing that has made for the most successful inductions will have tended to predominate through natural selection. Creatures inveterately wrong in their inductions have a pathetic but praise-worthy tendency to die before reproducing their kind.
>
> (Quine 1969, 126)

Something very important gets smuggled in here. Quine's expressions 'successful inductions' and 'wrong in their inductions' suggest that the inductive conclusions being drawn are either really true or really false, and that evolutionary success (or failure) depends on these inductions being true (or false). There are no grounds, however, for such a view. The spectrum example perfectly illustrates this. Beings who did *not* visually chop up the spectrum probably died for their beliefs – but they got it right.

Does Ruse identify truth with success? He puts the situation bluntly, but picturesquely:

> Pointing to the plausibility of the epigenetic-rule status of the sorts of things my position demands, let me make brief mention of the biological value of consilience. One hominid arrives at the water-hole, finding tiger-like foot prints at the edge, blood-stains on the ground, growls and snarls and shrieks in the nearby undergrowth, and no other animals in sight. She reasons: 'Tigers! Beware!' And she flees. The second hominid arrives at the water, notices all of the signs, but concludes that since all the evidence is circumstantial nothing can be proven. 'Tigers are just a theory, not a fact.' He then settles down for a good long

drink. Which one of these two hominids was your ancestor?

(*TDS*, 163)

I am sure we agree on which hominid is more likely to survive and reproduce. But notice that in answering this question we (and Ruse) implicitly assume that reasoning via consiliences really is correct reasoning and hence that it is what nature would select for. Ruse violates the spirit of his naturalism when he argues this way; he should instead say that reasoning in this fashion is correct *because it has been adaptive*, not that it is adaptive because it is correct. In Ruse's account the normative is not really eliminated after all. Standards of reasoning still exist, in platonic fashion, independently of us and independently of the processes of nature.

ETHICS

As with epistemology, Ruse distinguishes 'evolutionary' from 'Darwinian' ethics, and similarly, he rejects the former while embracing the latter. By 'evolutionary ethics' Ruse means that collection of views which are progressivist, especially Social Darwinism. Herbert Spencer, William Sumner and numerous other thoughtless people today still identify the good with the victor in the struggle to survive. Not only is this bad moral philosophy, it leads to some of the most pernicious views imaginable, such as Spencer's contention that 'organized charity [is] intolerable [since it] puts a stop to that natural process of elimination by which society continually purifies itself' (quoted in *TDS*, 74). Ruse rightly rejects all such evolutionary views of ethics. Either they beg the question by simply (without argument) identifying good with evolutionary progress; or they commit the naturalistic fallacy, i.e. they claim x *is* the case, therefore x *ought* to be the case. Or sometimes they argue that x is good because of its good consequences. While having good consequences might be laudable, the grounds for the ethical views in question are really utilitarian, which has naught to do with evolution.

As with epistemology, Ruse's positive view in ethics ('Darwinian ethics' as he calls it) is that we are in important respects hard-wired for certain basic sentiments. In particular, 'our moral sense is a biological adaptation, just like hands and feet' (*TDS*, 222). David Hume thought there is nothing more to ethics than the feelings we have toward our fellows. He remarked that 'Morality . . . is more properly felt than judg'd of' (*Treatise*, 470). Ruse explicitly endorses the Humean outlook, and thinks of himself as giving a genetic explanation for why we have these feelings. The great eighteenth-century naturalist held that:

> A man naturally loves his children better than his nephews, his nephews better than his cousins, his cousins better than strangers, where every thing else is equal. Hence arise our common measures of duty, in preferring one to the other. Our sense of Duty always follows the common and natural course of our passions.[4]

Ruse offers a genetic/evolutionary account of this 'natural' affection we have for our relations – Hume plus kin selection. 'Epigenetic rules giving us a sense of obligation have been put in place by selection, because of their adaptive value' (*TDS*, 223). This view is of a piece with the famous account of reciprocal altruism given by the sociobiologist Trivers: we practise the golden rule because it is adaptive.

The picture painted is somewhat bleak – a kind of moral nihilism. From the point of view of the universe, we really have no moral obligations at all to one another; there really is no such thing as right and wrong. Our genes cause us to have various feelings and sympathies, but there is no basis to morality beyond that. The worst that can be said about a man who murders his children is that his behaviour is not adaptive. (In some other environment it might be.)

Ruse asks a couple of questions which strike me as problematic: 'How do you compare and evaluate utilitarianism and the Darwinian position . . . ?' (*TDS*, 240) and 'which theory, Darwinism or utilitarianism, better accords with our moral feelings?' (*TDS*, 241). Neither question seems to be well-conceived. If he is generally right in offering a sociobiological account of morality, then presumably no action is truly right or wrong. Moral doctrines such as utilitarianism are simply irrelevant. Ruse's Darwinism is not a rival moral theory; it is an account of our behaviour, and as such it explains morality away. As for 'feelings', utilitarianism never tried to explain them anyway.

(Though it does try to do justice to moral sentiments taken as evidence, which is quite another matter.)

These issues are discussed in the light of Rawls's doctrine of reflective equilibrium. But I doubt its relevance here. Ruse's Darwinian account might still be right – and the rational thing to believe – even if it came off second best in a reflective equilibrium clash with utilitarianism or any other moral theory. In reflective equilibrium one tries to maximize the fit of moral theory with considered moral judgements; the latter are taken to be *prima facie* true moral judgements. The winning moral theory is the one which does justice to most of these. Ruse's Darwinian account says, in effect, this is a non-starter since there are no such things as *true moral judgements*.

Reflective equilibrium, taken as an evidential relation between any theory and some data, can be a useful device in evaluating Darwinism. However, Ruse's rivals are not other moral theories. Instead they are other theories which give, say, psychological accounts of the origin of moral feelings and behaviour. For example, the accounts of Freud (voice of the father) and Nietzsche (resentment) are Ruse's rivals; Kant, Mill and Rawls are not. To make this clear, let me draw an analogy. I believe unsupported objects fall. The theory of gravity explains why objects fall – but it does not explain why I believe that objects fall. To explain the latter I appeal to facts about myself, namely, that I have normal vision, that I have often been in the presence of falling bodies, etc. These beliefs about myself are not in conflict with the theory of gravity; two quite distinct things (why bodies fall and why I believe bodies fall) are being explained by two distinct theories.

Similarly, utilitarianism explains why, say, murder is wrong, while Ruse's Darwinism explains why we feel or believe it is wrong. Thus the conflict between the two is not head-on. But, as I already indicated, there can be an indirect conflict. It happens when the belief is false. For example, suppose I believe the pink elephant in front of me can float around the room. Why can it float? Explanation: Pink elephants possess levity. Why do I *believe* they can float? Explanation: I am in a drunken stupor. This second explanation undermines the first. Ruse's Darwinism (if right) undermines utilitarianism and Kantianism in the same indirect way. It is not a direct rival to these two moral theories in the way they are to each other.

69

For Ruse, morality is a kind of collective illusion foisted upon us by our genes. His account is for the ivory tower, not the market place, since he considers the illusion to be essential.

> The Darwinian argues that morality simply does not work (from a biological perspective), unless we believe that it is objective. Darwinian theory shows that, in fact, morality is a function of (subjective) feelings; but it shows also that we have (and must have) the illusion of objectivity. . . .

> (*TDS*, 253)

Ruse would like to think we can no more carry the truth about ethics from the seminar room to the street than Hume could carry his scepticism out of his study and into his daily life.

I am less sanguine than Ruse on the inevitability of felt objectivity in ethics. It is much more dubious in the case of morality than in the case of causality or induction. I have never met anyone under the influence of Hume who was willing to jump out of a window in the belief that maybe *this time* the laws of nature will be different. On the other hand, the world abounds with moral relativists who often as a result of their relativist beliefs display the most callous indifference toward the well-being of others. Ironically, we may find ourselves in the position of Mrs Wilberforce who, upon hearing about Darwin's theory that we are descended from apes, remarked 'Let us pray it is not true; but if it is, let us hope it does not become widely known'.

EVIDENCE

Why should we believe any of this? Ruse paints a pretty picture; this is what *Taking Darwin Seriously* is especially good at – presenting a coherent, naturalistic, evolutionary outlook which is plausible and attractive. In lieu of arguments, there are plenty of illustrative examples in this volume. Implicit arguments, however, permeate the book and can be easily teased out. Some of them are similar to the kinds of consideration one would offer for sociobiology, namely, claims about adaptability and universality, etc.

Adaptability

The opposable thumb, large brains and stereoscopic vision are obviously adaptive characteristics, so they would be selected for in the evolutionary process. Equally clearly, behaviour can be adaptive. Some kinds of activity will lead to having more offspring, others will lead to less. Thus, Ruse contends, nature selects for behaviour as well as for physical characteristics. Whether right or wrong, this is a standard sociobiological argument. Ruse extends it into the cognitive realm: nature selects for cognitive behaviour. Certain thought structures (both scientific and moral) are adaptive, so there is good reason to think they would be selected for in the evolutionary process. Just how adaptive typical human reasoning really is seems arguable. Kahneman and Tversky have chronicled a wide range of examples of common human reasoning which is sharply at odds with ordinary scientific reasoning (Kahneman et al. 1982). A typical example of this sort of 'faulty' reasoning goes something like this. The subject is asked about the probability of such and such (call it A) to which the evaluation given is, say, rather low. Then the subject is asked to give the probability of a somewhat longer story which includes A (call the whole thing A & B) to which the evaluation is very often higher than for A alone. These evaluations fly in the face of an elementary result from probability theory: $Prob(A \& B) < Prob(A)$. This situation seems to me to quite upset the Darwinian account, at least at one level.

First, suppose that scientific reasoning (which includes the just mentioned probability relation) is adaptive. Typical human reasoning violates this probability law; thus typical human reasoning is not adaptive. But if reasoning is genetically based, it must be both adaptive and (more or less) universal. Thus, no reasoning is genetically based; and so scientific reasoning isn't.

On the other hand, suppose that scientific reasoning is not adaptive (while allowing the possibility that common-sense reasoning is); then scientific reasoning is not genetically based. Either way, scientific reasoning is not innate.

Put another way, if science is adaptive, then what most people do much of the time is not; conversely, if our typical thought styles help us through life, then much of science has little to do with adaptive cognitive processes.

71

Universality

Universality is another standard ingredient in the sociobiological story. Some behaviours (e.g. incest taboos) seem to be universal. (Such examples are debatable, but let us grant them for now.) Consequently, it is unlikely that they are cultural products, but must instead be genetically based. Ruse's analogue in cognitive behaviour is that certain styles of scientific reasoning and certain moral feelings are universal, so they too must be genetically based and not a product of any culture. Universality, of course, does not provide knock-down evidence for a genetic basis. For example, it is universally believed that grass is green, yet neither Ruse nor anyone else thinks we are genetically determined to believe it. Perhaps the truth about both methodology and morals is platonic, and that certain elementary platonic facts are simply rather obvious so they can be seen (with the mind's eye) plainly by all; they are just as plainly seen as the fact that grass is green.

Few besides me will take the platonic alternative seriously, even though it accounts perfectly well for universality. An objection Ruse is more likely to hear is that there is *no* universality. Numerous philosophers of science (e.g. Kuhn, Laudan, Newton-Smith) claim that methodology is not a static enterprise, that it has developed through history. There was a time when people thought the only permissible way to do science was by deducing theories from empirical data. Ruse's favourite example, consiliences of induction, came into fashion in the nineteenth century, but was considered illegitimate before that. If this historical claim is right then the alleged universality of methodology, which is certainly needed for positing a genetic basis, is simply non-existent. The rug is thus pulled from under the Darwinian epistemologist's feet.

It is impossible to sort out these issues in brief compass, but I very much doubt the common assertion that methodology is a developing entity in spite of its manifest plausibility. Ruse has good instincts; the core of methodology is, I think, quite static[5] – though I favour an account of it along non-naturalist lines.

Making the Environment

Ruse's vision, like other epistemologists of an evolutionary bent, has individuals reacting to a given environment. What the vision seems insensitive to is the fact that organisms, to a very large extent, make the environment they live in. This is certainly true in the purely biological world, and I think it is also true in the realm of epistemology. Ironically, it is an analogy which undermines a Darwinian account of cognition. Instead of viewing organisms as having a fixed cognitive structure with which they passively grasp the world, we should instead conceive of them as actively imposing their own frameworks upon a world. That is, they try out different 'paradigms' or some such thing, and head back to the drawing board when the world resists.[6] The human mind on this view is indefinitely plastic; the Darwinian process has resulted not in a structured mind but in an unstructured one. Total flexibility in our thinking may, in fact, have greater survival value. If anything, the history of science, with its wildly divergent ways of conceptualizing the world, supports a plastic mind, not a hard-wired structure.

Reduction

Much of the motivation for any sort of naturalism stems from the desire to eliminate the normative. *Prima facie*, norms are queer things; they do not fit easily into a world consisting entirely of physical stuff. But there are different ways that norms can be reduced to the physical which, respectively, I shall call 'atomistic' and 'relational'. The first of these puts the principle of activity entirely within the basic entity of the reduction. Ruse, for example, puts the determination of cognitive structure into the individual person (where a person is nothing more than a complex physical system). The person's behaviour is then an *unfolding* of what has been built in. (When crudely interpreted, Liebniz's monadism is an extreme example of this.)

The other kind of naturalism also completely eliminates norms in favour of a purely physical ontology, but allows the behaviour of a person (which is again conceived to be just a complex physical system) to be the result of *relations* that person has with other physical objects, including other persons. In other words, a person's behaviour is not just the result of the genetic programme it was born with, but is also the product of its (physical) interaction with other (physical) beings, in short, with its environment. The recent naturalistic epistemologies of Richard Boyd and Larry Laudan[7] have this character. There is plenty of room to be a naturalist and a physicalist without being an innatist – one need only hold the relational version instead of the atomistic.[8]

Underdetermination

The evolutionary process does not settle everything. There is a large measure of underdetermination in Ruse's account.

> [A]s with scientific knowledge, no one is claiming that every last moral twitch is highly controlled by the genes. In science, the claim was that human reason has certain rough or broad constraints, as manifested through epigenetic rules. The application of these leads to the finished product, which in many respects soars into the cultural realm, transcending its biological origin. In the case of ethics, the Darwinian urges a similar position. Human moral thought has constraints, as manifested through the epigenetic rules, and the application of these leads to moral codes, soaring from biology into culture.
>
> (*TDS*, 223)

Ruse echoes Wilson's sentiment that genes have given up much of their sovereignty to culture. How much? It is hard to say, but his account is really rather modest in scope. Only a few methodological rules and moral sentiments are given a genetic treatment; most of what we do scientifically and ethically is the result of culture. This leaves a great deal of room for quite traditional concerns; e.g. should I try to maximize happiness (among those I am equally genetically related to)?; should I universalize (among those I am equally genetically related to)?; etc. These are issues left unsettled by genetic factors. Yet, we still want to know what their ontological status is. It has something to do with culture, but does this just mean that many moral rules are some sort of social convention? Or is a platonic account of the non-genetic residue correct? These remain open questions.

Ruse claims not to be an ethical relativist. '[U]niversality is guaranteed by the shared genetic background of every member of *Homo sapiens*. . . . There is, therefore, absolutely nothing arbitrary about morality . . .' (*TDS*, 255). This is half right. In so far as moral sentiments are genetically determined, we all have the same ones just as we all have ten toes. But in so far as there is much left undetermined by our genes, there is much room left for different systematizations. Of course, it is possible that genetically determined rules of logic etc. force a unique morality upon us, but given Ruse's liberality on the latter score, it seems most unlikely that we have anything like a unique outcome in ethics. So, should I share the last slice of pizza, or not?

An Alternative Picture

Any alternative to Ruse's Darwinian account must not fly in the face of some obvious facts. The human mind is a product of an evolutionary process, and some of the beliefs we have tend to be practically useful in surviving and reproducing. While conceding this view of our place in nature, at the same time I want to defend the view mentioned above, that our minds are indefinitely plastic. The tension can be resolved by appealing to a position long ago advocated by Wilfred Sellars.[9]

Sellars's *manifest image* is the common-sense conceptual framework that we all use. It includes red apples, tables made of solid continuous matter, people other than ourselves, hungry tigers etc. Sellars talks of the conceptual framework of the manifest image arising in the early dawn of time; but let us assume here that it is in fact genetically hard-wired within us. By contrast, the *scientific image* is being created right now. At present it embraces imperceptible atoms, electromagnetic fields, genes and uncaused events. In the scientific image there are no red apples since there are no colours, and there are no continuously solid tables since matter is not continuous. Consequently, there is a fundamental conflict between much of the manifest image and its counterpart in the scientific image.

Sellars assigns primacy to the scientific image, and so should we. If our concern is with reasonable belief, then we are concerned with the scientific image. But it is perfectly easy to see how the manifest image could have arisen in an evolutionary process which better enables us to survive.

The spectrum example I mentioned above perfectly illustrates the relation between the manifest and the scientific images. In the manifest image, we conceptualize the spectrum as composed of distinct intervals of colour, which seems quite proper, since this is how we actually perceive it. But in the scientific image, we conceptualize it as continuous. It is the clash of these two which tells us that the manifest image conceptualization of the spectrum is false, and moreover, that it is probably innate. Most especially, notice that we are not bound to conceptualize it as we do in the common-sense manifest image. The genetically determined framework can be transcended. (Many of the famous examples of fallacious thinking discussed by Kahneman and Tversky should be seen perhaps as instances of manifest image thinking – i.e. hard-wired thinking which is useful for survival.)

Are there no constraints on the scientific image? How plastic is the mind? I am inclined to say: no constraints at all; it is totally plastic. In support of this rather rash claim I want to try an argument I have not seen elsewhere, even though it is rather simple. It has to do with the nature of applied mathematics.

We already have set theory in our possession. In some important and relevant sense we can grasp it. When we do science, we in effect assert that some part of the physical world (or even the whole universe) has the same structure as some mathematical object. Since the realm of sets provides *all possible mathematical structures*, any way that the world could be is exactly isomorphic to some set-theoretic object. Since all of these mathematical structures are graspable in some relevant sense by the human mind, any way that the physical world could be is also graspable by the human mind. Of course, any alleged isomorphism between the physical world and some set-theoretic structure is a conjecture which may be false; science, after all, is very difficult and very fallible. But there is no way of thinking about physical reality which is ruled out by our genetically determined cognitive capacity, since (standard) set theory can provide the representation of any possible way reality might be. The mere fact that we possess set theory shows that there can be no (non-logical) constraints on our thinking.

I do not want to overdo the case against Ruse's naturalism. It would be wrong simply to dismiss the activity that goes by the name evolutionary or Darwinian epistemology. The biological, psychological and sociological information acquired is often of the highest importance. However, it should be seen for what it is, namely, the study of the structure of our manifest image. It has little or nothing to do with real epistemology which is the study of how the scientific image is being and ought to be constructed. (Notice that norms are still with us.) Konrad Lorenz endorses an evolutionary account of our cognitive structure which he took to be as Kant described. (Throw away the transcendental deduction, the categories are adaptive in this environment, but perhaps not in others.) Lorenz saw clearly the limitations of any genetic account of our thought processes. I shall close with his discussion of the issue which strongly suggests the distinction I have been urging between an everyday framework which is adaptive and another one – science – which can be slowly, carefully gleaned from nature.

The 'dots' produced by the coarse 'screens' used in the reproductions of photographs in our daily papers are satisfactory representations when looked at superficially, but cannot stand closer inspection with a magnifying glass. So, too, the reproductions of the world by our forms of intuition and categories break down as soon as they are required to give a somewhat closer representation of their objects, as is the case in wave mechanics and nuclear physics. All the knowledge an individual can wrest from the empirical reality of the 'physical world-picture' is essentially only a working hypothesis. And as far as their species-preserving function goes, all those innate structures of the mind which we call 'a priori' are likewise only working hypotheses.

(Lorenz 1941, 128)

5

PUTNAM'S VERIFICATION

It always seems to me extreme rashness on the part of
some when they want to make human abilities the
measure of what nature can do.

Galileo

If I were looking for a bumper sticker it would say, 'Let no one
join together what God hath put asunder'. Rorty has tried
to link truth with social consensus; Latour, facts with
Machiavellian politics; Ruse, knowledge with evolutionary
biology; and now Putnam wants to join rightness with rational
acceptability. But these are marriages made in hell.

PUTNAM'S PILGRIMAGE

Recent years have seen Hilary Putnam do a complete about-
face, going from paradigm realist to proselytizing anti-realist.
Putnam was one of the leaders away from the positivism and
logical empiricism which so dominated philosophy, especially
philosophy of science, well into the 1950s and 1960s. He has
been as responsible as anyone for the rejection of 'the received
view' (a phrase he coined) and the rise of scientific realism
during the 1960s and 1970s. As well as a general form of realism
(via such considerations as the miracle argument which he did
much to popularize), Putnam also argued strenuously and effectively for realism within the particular sciences: in quantum
mechanics, in space–time, in semantics, in the philosophy of
mind. But all that has changed.[1]

His new view – *anti-metaphysical realism*, as he calls it – is a
species of verificationism and is tied to 'human flourishing'.

Endorsing the view he attributes to Kant, Putnam says,

> a piece of knowledge (i.e. a 'true statement') is a statement that a rational being would accept on sufficient experience of the kind that it is actually possible for beings with our nature to have. 'Truth' in any other sense is inaccessible to us and inconceivable by us.
>
> (1981, 64)

Truth is no longer seen by Putnam as some sort of correspondence with reality; instead, it is tied to evidence. A statement is true if it is warrantedly assertible under ideal epistemic conditions. '[T]ruth is an *idealization* of rational acceptability' (1981, 55). If we are in ideal epistemic conditions and the evidence points to *p*, then *p must be true*. This contrasts with the metaphysical realist's view that all the evidence could point to *p* and yet *p* might still be false.

The view is clearly and avowedly anthropocentric. Putnam's verification procedures are quite explicitly tied to the human condition:

> Our conceptions of coherence and acceptability are, on the view I shall develop, deeply interwoven with our psychology. They depend upon our biology and our culture; they are by no means 'value free'. But they *are* our conceptions, and they are conceptions of something real. They define a kind of objectivity, *objectivity for us*, ...
>
> (1981, 55)

TRUTH AND RATIONAL ACCEPTABILITY

The case Putnam makes for his view is varied and often ingenious. One of Putnam's many arguments for his new view is the so-called brain-in-a-vat argument. Putnam imagines a brain in a vat, hooked up to a computer which gives it its various experiences. Normally, this sort of set-up would be used for a sceptical conclusion, but Putnam turns the argument around. Initially we are tempted to think that the brain is wrong when it thinks it is having a cheeseburger for lunch, even though, from the brain's perspective all the evidence points to the truth of 'I'm having a cheeseburger for lunch'. After all, it is really not eating anything. Our temptation is based on the assumption that it is possible that all the evidence points to the truth of p and yet p be false. This is certainly the view of realism and of common sense, but Putnam raises problems about reference. What does 'cheeseburger' mean to us, to the brain? For the brain the reference of 'cheeseburger' and 'eat' etc. is tied to the brain's experiences. It is not at all what we mean by these terms. So when the brain says 'I am eating a cheeseburger for lunch', this is to be interpreted in vat language, and it is then *not* false.

Another argument is based upon considerations drawn from mathematical logic. The Löwenheim–Skolem theorem says that any consistent first-order theory will have a countable model. Putnam asks us to suppose with the realist that truth and rational acceptability are distinct ideas, and that we have a theory, T, which is rationally acceptable but not true. We will further suppose that the world where T is false has countably many objects. It follows from the Löwenheim–Skolem theorem that there is an interpretation of T using the actual objects of the world, and in this interpretation T is true. So, the supposed distinction between truth and rational acceptability cannot be upheld after all.

This is only a sketch of Putnam's argument, and it doesn't really do justice to it. The glaring lacunae in my outline are not in Putnam's fleshed out version – but never mind, since the standard rejoinder which I shall now give doesn't turn on this at all. The usual reply to Putnam is based on the very plausible belief that the world is just too rich to allow the Löwenheim–Skolem theorem to apply. The theorem only works, for example, on first-order theories, ones in which the quantifiers are limited to ranging over individuals. But as soon as we allow propositions such as 'Socrates had all the qualities of a great philosopher' we move into the realm of second-order logic, where quantifiers range over properties as well as over individuals. 'Someone is wise' can be rendered: $(\exists x)\,Wx$, where W is the predicate 'is wise'. But 'Someone has all the properties of a great philosopher' must be rendered: $(\exists x)\,(\forall \phi)\,(P\,\phi \supset \phi x)$, where P is the predicate 'is a property of a great philosopher'. The fact that the quantifier ranges over all of these properties makes the Löwenheim–Skolem theorem inapplicable. Thus, Putnam's argument (suspect for various other reasons anyway) is undermined.

In spite of their cleverness, neither the brain-in-a-vat nor the model theoretic arguments seem to be Putnam's main reason for being an anti-realist. And rejecting them is not getting to the heart of Putnam's position. What does seem to be central is the deep anti-realist intuition (that some people just seem to be born with) that the only idea of truth we can have is one that is linked to how we actually determine what is true. ' "True" in any other sense is inaccessible to us and inconceivable by us' (1981, 64).

Putnam's claim that any other notion is 'inaccessible' and 'inconceivable' is highly reminiscent of the old 'we can't get outside our own heads to compare' claim of which Rorty made so much. Of course, it is not an argument in Putnam's hands any more than it was in Rorty's – but it is psychologically quite persuasive, nevertheless. It is, on the other hand, interesting to note that Putnam, who in the past has made so much of the distinction between conceivability and possibility ('It's conceivable that water isn't H_2O, but it's impossible'), should let anything important hang on our inability to conceive any other notion of truth. But I won't dwell on this point.

DEFINING REALISM

In the first chapter I gave a rough and ready characterization of *realism*. I shall now have to be a bit more precise. The definition of realism I like best overlaps with the definitions of several others (including Boyd, Dummett, Newton-Smith, Papineau, Putnam, Sellars and van Fraassen). It has three ingredients.

1 Theories are true or they are false, and what makes them true or false is something which exists completely independently from us.
2 We can make rational (though fallible) choices among rival theories.
3 Science aims at the truth.

A word or two about each. The first says that theories correspond to an independent reality. By 'independence' I mean that the truth of a theory has nothing to do with the structure of our minds (as it does for Kant) or the way we determine the truth-value of the theory (as it does for a verificationist).

Dummett's characterization of realism (1963, 146) is similar to (1), but that is clearly not enough. In *The Scientific Image*, van

Fraassen is happy to accept (1), but still calls himself an anti-realist. This is mainly because he rejects (2). He doesn't deny (or assert) the existence of micro-entities; rather, he is a sceptic when it comes to alleged knowledge of them – statements about electrons are really true or really false, but we can never know which. Thus, van Fraassen would reject (3) as well, since the aim of truth is hopeless. So, he is an anti-realist for epistemic, not ontological, reasons; Dummett, by contrast, is an anti-realist because he rejects (1).

There is one additional feature of (2) which it is important to stress. It does not say we can know everything; it only says that we can rationally choose between rival theories once they have been formulated. There is a small dose of humility involved. The motto for this chapter, taken from Galileo, endorsed (1). Galileo goes on in that passage to express a reverence for the inaccessible richness of the world; but he does not contradict (2); instead he complements it.

> It always seems to me extreme rashness on the part of some when they want to make human abilities the measure of what nature can do. On the contrary, there is not a single effect in nature, even the least that exists, such that the most ingenious theorist can arrive at a complete understanding of it.
>
> (*Dialogo*, 101)

The third ingredient in the definition of realism is there for several reasons, but I shall only mention one which is usually overlooked. Being a realist about a theory does not imply believing it is true. For example, I am a realist about the phlogiston theory, about the Genesis theory of creation and about classical mechanics. I consider them all false, known to be false, and yet I believe that their proponents had aimed for the truth. But think, for a moment, about a physicist who uses, say, classical mechanics (instead of relativity) or wave optics (instead of quantum optics) in his or her work. Realists maintain that these two theories have truth-values (false) and we have rational grounds for believing they are false. Has something gone wrong? Yes, in such a case condition (3) is violated. When classical mechanics is used to build a bridge or launch a satellite, it is only the empirical adequacy of the theory within the domain in question that matters. The aim of truth has been abandoned. And for such practical purposes this is often entirely appropriate. But in such cases we should understand that the theory is being used in an anti-realist way.

Returning now to Putnam, we can see that it is (1) (the independent reality criterion) that he rejects. He does not think there is a ready-made world out there that our theories either describe or fail to describe. Instead, what is the case is linked to how we determine what is the case. Putnam would strongly endorse (2) (we can make rational choices) and probably (3) (the aim is truth), though 'truth' will have to be understood in his anti-realist way. The reason he would be keen to endorse (2) is that he is at pains to distance himself from any sort of relativism. (We shall see below if he is successful.)

Although he abandons metaphysical realism, Putnam never-theless remains an 'internal realist', which he likens to being a scientific realist. What this comes to, I think, is simply that he puts statements about theoretical entities (e.g. electrons) on a par with statements about observational entities (e.g. streaks in cloud chambers). Statements about neither of these should be understood in the metaphysical realist way; but, on the other hand, there is no philosophically significant observational/theoretical distinction to be made concerning them. Theoretical electrons and observable streaks in cloud chambers are similarly dependent upon our verification methods; i.e. they are similarly dependent for their existence upon human biology, psychology and culture.

It is the distinction between (1) and (2) in the definition of realism which allows us to distinguish between the anti-realism of van Fraassen and the anti-realism of Putnam. Let us keep this in mind when we look now at an old argument of Sellars.

INTERNAL REALISM

In light of his internal realism, Putnam should be sympathetic to the following consideration due to Wilfred Sellars which is one of the more effective arguments for scientific realism (or internal realism). It occurs in his classic article 'The language of theories' (1961). We are asked to imagine a sample of gold dissolving in *aqua regia* at a rate r. The explanation of this phenomenon is simple: this is a bit of gold and all gold dissolves in *aqua regia* at rate r. Now imagine a second bit of gold that dissolves at a different rate; i.e. imagine a second bit of stuff which is identical to gold in every *observable* way *except* that it dissolves at the rate r'. It is at this point, says Sellars, that we must introduce theoretical entities. We posit a micro-structure and use that to explain the different rates of dissolving.

If there was some observable difference, say weight per volume, between the two bits of gold, then there would be no motivation or justification for introducing a micro-structure. We would simply explain things this way: this is a bit of *light* gold and all light gold dissolves at rate r, and that is a bit of *heavy* gold and all heavy gold dissolves at rate r'. (I am making the false but harmlessly simplifying assumption that there is no other kind of evidence for a micro-structure than the considerations given in this example.)

Two features of the Sellars argument must be stressed. We do not posit theoretical entities to explain empirical generalizations, but rather to explain why those generalizations sometimes fail. And second, if there had been only one type of gold, and hence only one rate of dissolving, then *there would have been no motivation or justification for positing a micro-structure*. It follows from this that if we had lived in a possible world with only one type of gold then we would have no evidence for postulating theoretical entities.

The preceding considerations should be perfectly congenial (at least in principle) to Putnam; they are of a piece with his internal realism. The considerations which are to follow immediately should also be congenial since they are just the views he shares with Kripke (1972) on necessity and natural kinds. (He now understands this doctrine in an anti-metaphysical realist way, but that will have no bearing on the following.)

NATURAL KINDS

The Putnam–Kripke doctrine of natural kinds goes roughly like this. We pick things out such as water or gold by pointing to samples or by describing them in observable terms. These observable characteristics, however, are not what is meant by 'water' or by 'gold', or by any other natural kind term. Putnam (1975c) asks us to consider Twin-Earth where everything is the same except that what they call 'water' is really made of XYZ instead of H_2O. That is, everything looks the same and acts the same; even the mental states of the Twin-Earthers are the same as ours. The only difference is in the micro-structure of the two substances.

Since water is made of H_2O, the stuff on Twin-Earth, says Putnam, is not water. In any possible world in which there is water, it is H_2O. This is a necessary truth. The same goes for all natural kinds; gold, for example, necessarily has a micro-structure which gives it atomic number 79.

For the sake of the argument, let us assume that the Putnam–Kripke theory of natural kinds is true. Further, let us assume that we are in ideal epistemic conditions and that we have evidence that gold has micro-structure M (and the isotope has structure M'). Since the evidence supports this in ideal conditions, by Putnam's account of truth, it must be *true* that gold has micro-structure M (and the isotope M'). Therefore, in every possible world (in which they exist) gold has micro-structure M (and the isotope has M'). But if it is true that gold has micro-structure M in possible world W, then under ideal epistemic conditions there must be evidence in W that this is so. By the Sellars argument above, there is evidence for a micro-structure only if there are both types of gold. Thus, in world W both types of gold must exist. If one type of gold is present then the other *must* be present in that possible world too.

Obviously, this is absurd. The combined presence of both types of gold is a contingent matter, if ever there was one. If we hold fast to the contingency of the presence of both types of gold and so to the contingency of experience – as I am sure we must – then we are compelled to say this: there are possible worlds where there is only one type of gold; that it has micro-structure M; but that even in ideal epistemic conditions in that world, there is no evidence that it has any micro-structure at all.

This consideration breaks Putnam's link between truth and evidence, and with it goes his verificationism.

RELATIVISM

No one familiar with the amazing achievements and spectacular progress of the natural sciences has a kind word for relativism. And rightfully so. This is as true of the new Putnam, the anti-realist, as it was of the old Putnam who used 'truth' to explain the success of science. At every turn he is at pains to distance himself from those who cheerfully fall into relativism.

> If one says (as Rorty recently has) that rightness is simply a matter of what one's 'cultural peers' would agree to, or worse, that it is defined by the 'standards of one's culture' (Rorty compares these to an algorithm), then the question can immediately be put: Do the standards of Rorty's culture (which he identifies as 'European culture') really require Rorty's 'cultural peers' to assent to what he has written? Fortunately, the answer is negative. Extreme versions of relativism are inconsistent in more than one way, as Plato saw. It is important to recognize, as Kuhn came to do, that rationality and justification are presupposed by the activity of criticizing and inventing paradigms and are not themselves defined by any single paradigm. Kuhn's move away from relativism is one that I hail.
>
> (1984, 121)

But how does Putnam, himself, avoid falling into the very relativism he rightly despises? With 'independent reality' banished, how is it possible to maintain the distinction that objectivity demands, the distinction between 'being right' and merely 'thinking we are right'?

The problem is partly solved by Putnam's notion of 'ideal epistemic conditions'. Under such conditions, 'being right' and 'thinking we are right' collapse into the same thing – that's what it means to be a verificationist. But in non-ideal conditions (which is what, for practical purposes, we are always in) the distinction holds up: we could all believe p and still be wrong.

There is a temptation to grumble about the notion of 'ideal epistemic conditions'. After all, didn't Putnam dismiss 'truth' in the realist's sense as 'inaccessible and inconceivable'? Is there a difference between a 'God's-eye-view' and 'ideal epistemic conditions'? Perhaps, but just barely. Putnam likens the latter to frictionless planes. We never quite realize either, but we can make very good approximations.

It is an interesting analogy, but rather doubtful. How do we know a plane is (approximately) frictionless? Because a body of mass m moving on the plane undergoes (approximately) zero acceleration. In other words, we are using the law $F = ma$ to determine whether the plane is indeed frictionless. (The chain of inference is simply this: since $a = 0$, it follows that $ma = 0$; therefore $F = 0$; and consequently there are no frictional forces, since there are no forces at all; thus, the plane is frictionless.) But after reasoning in this way we can hardly turn around and use the frictionless plane to test the law $F = ma$. (The air tracks of the undergraduate physics lab *illustrate* this law, they do not test it.)

Analogously, we would have to use some epistemological theory which tells us what is and what is not evidentially relevant to determine whether we are indeed in ideal epistemic conditions. There is a kind of circularity involved in both cases. It is not a vicious circle, but it is a circle, nevertheless; and it cannot be used in any non-question-begging way. Those who worry about the God's-eye-view metaphor should worry about ideal epistemic conditions, too. (For my part, I am worried about neither.)

Even if 'ideal epistemic conditions' proves to be a workable notion, it still isn't enough to ward off relativism. In addition we need to be assured that our theories are (approximately) true or are approaching the truth (i.e. where truth is rational acceptability under ideal epistemic conditions). It won't do to have people's beliefs all over the map with no hope of convergence. But convergence is what Putnam guarantees with his idea of 'human flourishing'. Objectivity for Kant is based on a kind of transcendent rationality – not just humans, but any rational being has to think in such and such a way. But for Putnam, things are much more tied to the contingent details about us. Putnam's notions of coherence and acceptability are 'deeply interwoven with our psychology. They depend upon our biology and our culture. . . . They define a kind of objectivity, *objectivity for us . . .*' (1981, 55). I suppose the ideas of biological and psychological flourishing are clear enough, but this seems a mighty slender thread on which to hang rationality. And it is only clear as long as we do not press for precise details; those who work in bioethics know how problematic 'health', 'disease' etc. are. One can easily imagine rival biological and psychological theories which lead to rival conceptions of human flourishing, and these in turn lead to different versions of ideal epistemic conditions, culminating in quite different theories being rationally acceptable (i.e. true). It is far from certain that invoking 'human flourishing' will help in the least to put relativism to rest.

A FINAL NOTE

I have used Putnam's theory of reference to attack his verificationism. But I am not entirely happy with that theory, so I want
now to briefly say why. In doing so, I realize that to some extent
I undermine my own argument against Putnam.

Putnam says that the principle at work in the baptism of water
is this:

> x is water if and only if it bears the relation *is the same liquid
> as* to this (pointing to a sample of water in the actual
> world).

Thus, if water turns out to be H_2O, then anything else is water
just in case it is also H_2O. But how are we to understand the
relation, 'is the same liquid as'? Without any comment, Putnam
(and Kripke, too) take it to mean 'has the same micro-structure
as'. But this is an unexamined prejudice. Given the enormous
success of the scientific revolution and its mechanical, efficient-
causes-only, account of nature this is surely the right prejudice
to have – about the *actual* world. But if we are allowed to include
a possible world as well, then this simply won't do.

There may be a possible world governed by quasi-Aristotelian
teleological and functional laws. The essence of a thing in such a
world has to do with the role it plays, not with its micro-
structure. Thus, the essence of 'water' in such a world is connected to the fact that it (let us suppose) nourishes plants and
animals there. In such a possible world 'is the same liquid as'
means something like 'plays the same functional role as'.
Having the same micro-structure would be merely accidental.

Let us suppose now that 'water' in our world is H_2O and in
theirs it is XYZ, but that in both worlds it plays the same
functional role of nourishing plants and animals etc. Their scientists would *correctly* say that their 'water' and ours *are the same
liquid*; our scientists would *correctly* say that they are different
liquids. And that's absurd.

Part III

MIRRORS

I began by painting a realist picture of science, then turned my attention to some of the anti-realists. It is time to stop grumbling and to return to the realist image. What I am *not* going to do is try to give further arguments for realism in general – that debate is pretty much exhausted. Rather, I am interested in some of the details of the metaphysics and epistemology of science, as I see them. The balance of this book will focus on the role of abstraction, abstract objects and a priori ways of getting at reality.

A brief chapter on laws of nature and thought experiments comes first. Some of the wonderful (often a priori) ways in which thought experiments work will be described. (This chapter draws on my earlier book, *The Laboratory of the Mind: Thought Experiments in the Natural Sciences* (1991), to which readers may turn for further details.) The next in this group of chapters is about 'phenomena', a relatively abstract sort of thing, to be sharply distinguished from observational data. The chapter on the vector potential in electrodynamics is rather technical; it can really only be understood by those with some background in physics. Nevertheless, I include it here to illustrate the importance of considering abstract entities in working physics. Our understanding of the minutiae of physical theory can be influenced by our attitude toward abstract objects, and conversely, the case for particular abstract objects must be made through consideration of the details of those very theories. Readers without the appropriate background can skip this chapter, though most of it should be accessible. The final chapter takes up the issue of platonism in mathematics in the light of Lakatos's fallibilism. To what extent, if any, are they compatible?

PART III

These four chapters are part of a research programme which has the aim of determining the role and the extent of abstract entities in science. This theme was taken up in my earlier book, *The Laboratory of the Mind*, and I expect to continue it in the future.

6

KNOWLEDGE –
IN THE ABSTRACT

LAWS OF NATURE

Scientists search for the laws of nature. That seems an innocuous claim, yet many philosophers deny it, or at least qualify it half to death. Van Fraassen (1989) thinks it is impossible, because there are no laws of nature. His is an extreme view, but it is in the long empiricist tradition from David Hume to David Lewis. It is a tradition that denies the existence of anything over and above the objects and events of the world themselves. John Earman has laid down the 'empiricist loyalty test' which involves subscribing to the principle that if two possible worlds agree on all the occurrent facts then they agree on the laws. He rightly claims that this principle 'captures the central empiricist intuition that laws are parasitic on occurrent facts' (Earman 1986, 85). He's right about empiricism, but is he right about laws?

The alternative is some sort of realist view, a view which takes laws of nature to be real things in their own right. This is not the only alternative, but it is the one worth pursuing. It has been championed in recent years by David Armstrong (1983), Fred Dretske (1977) and Michael Tooley (1977, 1988). They differ significantly in some details, but the general idea is the same: a law of nature is a relation between universals. Tooley's version is the most platonic and the one which seems to me the most likely right. Though I shall speak of them generically, it is Tooley's account that I have mainly in mind. (To adapt Pope's famous couplet: Cause and Nature's Laws lay hid by night; God said 'Let Tooley be!' and all was light.)

Let's begin with an extended example, the taxonomy known

91

as the *standard model* of elementary particles. I shall argue that only a realist account of laws can do justice to this paradigm piece of scientific work.

The standard model is an elegant and powerful taxonomy which has come into existence over the past twenty years. The basic assumption is that matter consists of two types of particles, quarks and leptons, and that there are forces between them which are carried by a third type of particle known as bosons. There are a variety of quarks (up, down, charmed, strange, truth, beauty) which combine in various ways to form the more familiar protons and neutrons. The leptons include the electron, the various neutrinos, the muon, etc. The bosons include the photon (which carries the force for electrical interactions), the vector bosons (which carry the weak force) and gluons (which carry the strong force). Gravitation has resisted all efforts to be successfully incorporated, but it is thought there should be gravitons to carry the gravitational force, as well.

The amazing thing about quarks and leptons is that they come in families. The first family consists of the up (u) and down (d) quarks, and of the electron (e^-) and the neutrino which is associated with the electron (v_e). Then at a much higher energy level comes a second family consisting of the charmed (c) and the strange (s) quarks, and of the muon (μ) and the muon-neutrino (v_μ). Again at a yet higher energy level we find the quarks truth (t) and beauty (b) (sometimes called top and bottom), the tauon (τ) and the tau-neutrino (v_τ). Table 1 makes this perspicuous.

Table 1

	First family	Second family	Third family	Fourth family	Fifth family	?
Leptons	e^-	μ	τ	?	?	?
	v_e	v_μ	v_τ	?	?	?
Quarks	u	c	t	?	?	?
	d	s	b	?	?	?

High energy physicists are perfectly confident of these three families (though the t quark has yet to be detected). A fourth and even a fifth family are being investigated, though obviously much will be settled only with the construction of even more powerful accelerators. But the inclination to assume ever more families of particles is extremely natural. For one thing, the masses of the particles grow from family to family in a roughly regular way. The masses of the quarks (expressed in units of MeV/c^2) are u, 5; d, 8; c, 1,270; s, 175; b, 4,250; the mass of t is unknown; all the neutrinos are probably of mass 0, but this remains an open question; e, 0.5; μ, 105; and τ, 1,784. When we look at the table of particle families, it seems perfectly obvious that the only thing standing in the way of finding heavier quarks and leptons is the lack of energy. From a practical point of view we could never get beyond a fifth or sixth family, and given the finiteness of the universe we could never, in principle, get beyond the nth family, for some finite number n. Yet it would seem that the classification scheme does not stop there. It goes on indefinitely. The taxonomy, of course, embodies laws of nature. Thus, 'the mass of the u quark is 5 MeV/c^2' is an example of a law. Just as the taxonomy goes on forever, so do the laws about ever heavier quarks and leptons, even though they are never instantiated. Now let's look at empiricist views of laws of nature to see how they handle this example.

'All events seem entirely loose and separate' says Hume. 'One event follows another, but we never can observe any tie between them' (*Enquiry*, 74). '[A]fter a repetition of similar instances, the mind is carried by habit, upon the appearance of one event, to expect its usual attendant, and to believe that it will exist' (*Enquiry*, 75). Causality and the laws of nature are each nothing more than mere regularities. To say that fire causes heat or that it is a law of nature that fire is hot is to say nothing more than that fire is constantly conjoined with heat. Hume defined cause as 'an object, followed by another, and where all the objects similar to the first are followed by objects similar to the second' (*Enquiry*, 76).[1] We cannot see a 'connection' between fire and heat such that if we knew of the one we could know that the other must also occur. All we know is that whenever in the past we have experienced one we have also experienced the other. Hence, the 'regularity' or 'constant conjunction' view of causality and laws of nature.

The appeal to empiricists is evident. All that exists are the regular events themselves; there are no mysterious connections between events – no metaphysics to cope with. The general form of a law is simply a universal statement. 'It is a law that As are Bs' has the form $(\forall x)(A x \supset B x)$; 'it is a law that u quarks have mass 5' comes to: all u quarks have mass 5.

There are two general problems with this view. The first problem is that the simple regularity view makes too many things into laws. For instance, while writing this in my study I have socks on and so do my children; no one else is in my office. Thus, it is true that all the people in my office are wearing socks. It has the form of a law according to the regularity account. But obviously it isn't. So the simple version is usually supplemented with an extra ingredient to distinguish genuine laws from 'accidental' generalizations. Hume's laws are regularities that we have expectations about, expectations built on habit. Among contemporaries who adopt such a subjective view of laws is Nelson Goodman, who remarks, 'we might say a law is a true sentence used for making predictions. . . . [R]ather than a sentence being used for prediction because it is a law, it is called a law because it is used for prediction . . .' (1947, 20). From 'All ravens are black' I am willing to predict that the next raven I see will also be black; but from 'All people in my study are wearing socks' I wouldn't bet too heavily that the next person to enter my office will be wearing socks. And A. J. Ayer's 'suggestion is that the difference between our two types of generalization lies not so much on the side of the facts which make them true or false, as in the attitude of those who put them forward' (1956, 88).

This has some unsavoury consequences. If different people were to adopt different attitudes to the various generalizations, it would mean they had different laws – and no one could be said to be wrong. Thus R. B. Braithwaite 'makes the notion of natural law an epistemological one and makes the "naturalness" of each natural law relative to the rational corpus of the thinker' (1953, 317). As well as the relativity of laws on this subjective account, there is another unpalatable consequence. Before there were sentient beings who could adopt different attitudes to various generalizations, there were no laws of nature at all.

So the first class of problems with the regularity view has to do with its making too many things laws of nature, and the way it treats that problem is by turning laws into subjective entities. The second class of problems has to do with the regularity view's inability to do justice to the example above, the standard model of particle physics. And the reason is simple. There are no regularities in nature that are instances of the higher families. For some n, it will be impossible to have instances of quarks and leptons of the nth family realized in nature because of the lack of energy in the universe. Yet there are laws that describe the masses of these very heavy particles.

It won't do to shrug this off with the observation that a ∀-statement with a false antecedent is true. For laws support counter-factuals. The statement 'If an x quark had interacted with an electron then p would be true' is supported by the genuine law about x quarks, and not by just any vacuously true sentence.

A variation on the Humean theme which does justice to Earman's loyalty test has been proposed by Frank Ramsey and (following Ramsey) by David Lewis. Laws, on this account, are propositions at the heart of any systematization of the facts of nature (regularities or not). Ramsey writes that 'causal laws [are] consequences of those propositions which we should take as axioms if we knew everything and organized it as simply as possible in a deductive system' (1931, 242). Ramsey only held the view for a short time since 'it is impossible to know everything and organize it in a deductive system'. But David Lewis (1973) rightly pointed out that this is a poor reason to reject the view, since we can talk about the ideal systematization (one which best combines simplicity and strength) without knowing what it is.

In brief, this account supposes there are different ways of systematically describing the events in the history of the universe. Some of these will be simpler than others; some more powerful than others. One of these is assumed to best combine simplicity with power, though we may have no idea which it is. The most powerful system of axioms would imply every event. We can get this by making every statement that describes an event one of the axioms. Obviously, this won't be very simple. Extremely simple systems would have very few laws. The Ramsey–Lewis view envisages the optimal combination of strength and simplicity; the statements of that system and their logical consequences are the laws of nature. Presumably, '$F = ma$' (or things like it) would be a consequence of such an ideal systematization, and hence a law, while 'There is no pizza left' wouldn't, and so would be one of life's sad little contingencies.

Like the naive regularity account, laws of nature on the

Ramsey–Lewis view do *not* explain anything. Laws, on both views, are supervenient, they are like summary descriptions. But far from seeing this as an objection, empiricists cheerfully embrace the fact, since laws, as Earman sees it, are parasitic on events. More to the credit of the Ramsey–Lewis view is the way it overcomes the objections raised above that laws of nature are subjective, relative to belief systems, or that they were non-existent before humans came on the scene. Since ideal systematizations (to any platonist-minded logician) exist quite independently of us, none of the subjectivity of the Humean view remains. (There is the worry that 'simplicity' is itself a subjective notion, but let's not be concerned with this here.) Even though the problems stemming from subjectivity are overcome, one big problem remains. We return, once again, to the standard model.

If our interest is in systematizing the occurrent events of the universe, then the maximally simple and powerful system will contain axioms describing the families of particles up to the nth, for some finite n, and no higher. Any axiom describing x quarks (where x quarks are from a family higher than n) would never imply any event that happens in the universe. It would imply more things, but not more things that actually happen. So the simplicity ingredient rules such an axiom out of the ideal systematization. On the Ramsey–Lewis view, there just aren't laws of nature describing families higher than the nth. But, of course, there are such laws, so the Ramsey–Lewis view is missing them. There is more to a law of nature than a regularity or a description of a set of occurrent facts, and that something more is not captured either by subjective attitudes or by ideal deductive systematizations – that something extra must be in reality itself.

A new account of laws is the simultaneous, independent creation of David Armstrong, Fred Dretske and Michael Tooley. Each claims that laws of nature are relations among universals, i.e. among abstract entities which exist independently of physical objects, independently of us and outside of space and time. It is, at least in Tooley's version, a species of platonism.

The 'basic suggestion', according to Tooley, 'is that the fact that universals stand in certain relationships may logically necessitate some corresponding generalization about particulars, and that when this is the case, the generalization in question expresses a law' (1977, 672).

A law is not a regularity, it is rather a link between properties. When we have a law that Fs are Gs we have the existence of universals, F-ness and G-ness, and a relation of necessitation between them. (Armstrong symbolizes it as $N(F, G)$.) A regularity between Fs and Gs is said to hold in virtue of the universals F and G. '[T]he phrase "in virtue of universals F and G" is supposed to indicate,' says Armstrong, that 'what is involved is a real, irreducible, relation, a particular species of the necessitation relation, holding between the universals F and G . . .' (1983, 97). The law entails the corresponding regularity, but is not entailed by it. Thus we have:

$$N(F, G) \rightarrow (\forall x)(Fx \supset Gx).$$

And yet:

$$(\forall x)(Fx \supset Gx) \nrightarrow N(F, G).$$

The relation N of nomic necessity is understood to be a primitive notion, a theoretical entity posited for explanatory reasons. N is also understood to be contingent which at first sight seems a contradiction. How can a relation of necessitation be contingent? Answer: In this world Fs are required to be Gs, but in other worlds Fs may be required to be something else. The law $N(F, G)$ is posited only for this world; in other possible worlds perhaps a different law, $N(F, G')$, holds.

Some of the advantages of a realist view of laws are immediately apparent. To start with, this account distinguishes – objectively – between genuine laws of nature and accidental generalizations. Second, laws are independent of us – they existed before we did and there is not a whiff of relativism about them. Thus, they can be used to *explain* and not merely to describe events. But most important, notice the justice it does to our intuitive understanding of the standard model. Laws on the platonic view are not parasitic on existing objects and events. They have a life of their own. Even if the universe should not have enough energy within it to produce very heavy quarks and leptons, there can still be laws about such things.

This last point can be used to distinguish between realist alternatives. Tooley, as I mentioned, holds the most platonic version of the various realist accounts. Armstrong, who wants to be as much of a naturalist as he can be, holds (with Aristotle) that un-instantiated universals do not exist. (If there were no red things, there would be no redness.) The standard model clearly points in Tooley's direction, for it is perfectly clear that there could be laws about ever heavier quarks, even though those laws, in principle, will never be instantiated.

The standard model has proved a very powerful example. Why? I suspect that it is because within it we see a pattern of patterns, a regularity among regularities. The laws of nature describing the particles within any single family could be viewed as a mere regularity, in the way an empiricist would view any other regularity, and with as much or little success. But over and above this we see a regularity among the distinct families of particles, a second-order regularity. It is this which makes the standard model unusual and gives it its power. For it seems we must take the regularities within a family seriously, ontologically, as things in their own right, in order to make sense of the second-order regularities. A crude analogy from set theory may help. We often point to a flock of birds and say 'That's a set of birds'. To a first approximation this is right; we harmlessly identify the physical collection a, b, c with the set $\{a, b, c\}$. But pretty quickly in set theory we want to distinguish sets of objects from sets of sets of objects. In particular, $\{\{a, b, c\}\}$ is quite distinct from $\{a, b, c\}$, and so cannot be also harmlessly reduced to the physical collection a, b, c. Among the truths we insist on are that $\{a, b, c\}$ has three elements, while $\{\{a, b, c\}\}$ has only one. Once we start the hierarchy of sets we start taking them seriously as entities in their own right, and then we're on the royal road to Plato's heaven (and a good thing, too). I suspect that something like this happens when we notice the pattern of patterns in the standard model, for the second-order pattern cannot be reduced to the first-order pattern among actual objects and events any more than a set of sets can.

KNOWLEDGE OF LAWS

When we know a law of nature, we know something about the physical world, but we also know something about the abstract realm; we know that such and such a relation exists between properties. This is our knowledge – in the abstract.

According to Armstrong, Dretske and Tooley, their view of the laws of nature is pure metaphysics. It gives an account of the nature of laws and explains the regularities which obtain. However, the way we *learn* about laws is the same for them as it is for the staunch empiricists: we look at individual instances of the regularity; we see ravens, never ravenhood. I want to add an epistemological aspect to this metaphysical account of laws. It seems a shame to have all this metaphysical apparatus around and not put it to epistemological work. The claim I shall try to defend is this: in very special circumstances *we can see the laws of nature* – not the regularities, but the abstract patterns themselves. This gives us a priori knowledge of the physical world. In what special circumstances? In thought experiments; that's when we see into the abstract realm. But I shall get to this later; first we need some stage-setting.

The view I propose is not unlike platonism in mathematics. Recently Roger Penrose took up the cudgels for mathematical platonism when he remarked: 'whenever the mind perceives a mathematical idea, it makes contact with Plato's world of mathematical concepts. . . . When one "sees" a mathematical truth, one's consciousness breaks through into this world of ideas, and makes direct contact with it . . .' (1989, 428). There are several ingredients involved in platonism, including: (1) there are abstract objects existing outside of space and time; (2) the way these objects are is what makes our mathematical statements true or false; (3) the mind can grasp, see or intuit (some of) them; (4) our mathematical knowledge is a priori in the sense of being independent of the physical senses, but it need not be infallible.

Gödel, the foremost platonist of recent times, writes

despite their remoteness from sense experience, we do have something like a perception also of the objects of set theory, as is seen from the fact that the axioms force themselves upon us as being true. I don't see any reason why we should have any less confidence in this kind of perception, i.e., in mathematical intuition, than in sense perception.

(1947, 484)

the assumption of such objects is quite as legitimate as the assumption of physical bodies and there is quite as much reason to believe in their existence. They are in the same sense necessary to obtain a satisfactory system of mathematics as physical bodies are necessary for a satisfactory theory of our sense perceptions. . . .

(1944, 456f.)

99

I won't argue for platonism in mathematics here. (See my 1991 book for a defence.) But given the truth of platonism in mathematics, and given that Tooley *et al.* have hit on the right metaphysical account of laws of nature, should we not expect actually to get a glimpse of those laws? In fact, would it not be a bit surprising if we were not able to somehow or other perceive them?

Of course, the platonism in physics that I am sketching faces the same objections commonly made against Gödel; namely, how is such a 'grasping' or 'perception' possible, since abstract objects, being outside of space and time, cannot causally interact with us? Meeting this objection largely amounts to showing that the causal theory of knowledge is wrong, at least if it means *physical* causation. My case for knowledge (including a priori knowledge) of laws as abstract entities can only stand up if this very popular, naturalistic account of knowledge is seen to be deeply wrong. The next few sections are devoted to showing this.

CAUSAL EMPIRICISM

Contemporary empiricism is closely allied with naturalism. Not only do empiricists hold that all our knowledge is based upon sensory experience, but they also tend to offer some sort of causal account of how this experience comes about.[2] The causal ingredient in knowledge seems very plausible – after all, my knowing that there is a tea cup on my desk is based on sense impressions which are caused by the cup itself. Photons come from the cup to my eye; a signal is then sent down the optic nerve into the visual part of the brain, and so on. And without that causal process, I probably wouldn't have the sensations that I do have.

It would seem not unfair, then, to characterize contemporary empiricism as holding:

> Knowledge of X is based on sensory experience for which there is an underlying physical causal connection between the knower and X; there are no other sources of knowledge.

It might seem that *causal empiricism* (as I shall call it) is more restrictive than earlier forms of empiricism. I suppose it is in that knowledge requires a causal connection in addition to sensory experience. But the causal ingredient is a very natural comp-lement to the older empiricism and fits in very well with other views that are all the rage, such as causal theories of reference, causal decision theory etc.

Such a doctrine would seem to do complete justice to a very wide range of cases. As well as mundane cup-on-the-table-in-front-of-me examples, causal empiricism easily handles the unobservable. On this account we know about electrons, for instance, because we have appropriate sense experience of white streaks in cloud chambers and because that very experi-ence is causally connected via the white streaks to electrons themselves. (Being electrically charged, they ionize the water molecules in the cloud chamber which in turn emit light in the visible part of the spectrum etc. The causal chain from electron to brain is easily established.)

Similarly, we can know about the future. This morning's cloud formations caused a sensation in me that leads me to believe (at noon) that it will rain later tonight. Those very cloud formations this morning are the cause of tonight's rain. So not only do I have the relevant sensory experience, but I am also causally connected to the future rain – not directly connected, of course, but indirectly connected via this morning's clouds. (These clouds are said to be 'the common cause' of both the rain and my belief that it will rain.)

A caution about the causal connection is required. The thesis is only that such a connection must exist in order for there to be knowledge. Of course, it must be the right sort of connection, but for our purposes I shall only be concerned with what causal empiricism sees as the necessary, not sufficient, conditions for knowledge. Knowing what the appropriate connection might be is certainly not required. Our ancestors, for instance, knew about cups on tables long before they knew about photons.

With this account of contemporary empiricism in mind, we can formulate an appropriate characterization of a priori knowledge:

> Knowledge of X is a priori if and only if it is knowledge which is independent of any causally based sense-experience.

Causal empiricists, given this definition, will say that a priori knowledge is impossible. Indeed, a characterization like this, stressing the causal aspect, is what empiricists have in mind when they attack mathematical platonism. They argue as follows: since mathematical objects are abstract entities outside of space and time, there can be no causal connection between them and us; therefore, even if they did exist, they would be unknowable, in principle.[3] Exactly the same argument can be made against the realist view of laws of nature: since laws (on this view) are abstract entities, outside of space and time, they cannot causally interact with us; thus, even if they did exist, they would be unknowable, in principle. The moral in either case is that we should abandon the platonic account.

Let's now look at a piece of amazing physics to see whether this argument is effective.

EPR AND THE BELL RESULTS

The makers of quantum mechanics (QM) understood their formalism in a rather straightforward, classical way.[4] Erwin Schrödinger, for example, thought of the $||\psi\rangle|^2$ in his equation as representing a physical entity, say, an electron which he conceived as a wave, more or less spread out in space. On the other hand, Max Born proposed that $||\psi\rangle|^2$ should be understood as the probability density for the location of an electron. In his view the electron is a particle; the state vector $|\psi\rangle$ just tells us the probability amplitude of its being located at various places. The waves of so-called wave–particle duality are probability waves – they are a reflection of our ignorance, not of the physical world itself which is made of localized particles existing independently of us.

We can think of Schrödinger's view as an ontological interpretation of QM, since $|\psi\rangle$ is about the world, and Born's as an epistemological interpretation, since $|\psi\rangle$ is about our knowledge of the world. Since neither of these philosophically straightforward interpretations works, the attractiveness of the anti-realist Copenhagen approach becomes somewhat inevitable. The Copenhagen interpretation is mainly the product of Niels Bohr, though there are numerous variations. Bohr thought the wave and particle aspects of any physical system are equally real; $|\psi\rangle$ has both ontological and epistemological ingredients. As Heisenberg put it, 'This probability function represents a

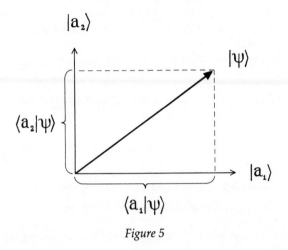

Figure 5

mixture of two things, partly a fact and partly our knowledge of a fact' (1958, 45). A state of superposition, on this view, is not a mere state of ignorance – *reality itself is indeterminate*. An electron, for example, does not have a position or a momentum until a position or a momentum measurement is made; the very act of measuring makes the magnitude measured. In classical physics (as standardly understood), observations *discover* reality, but in QM, according to Bohr and Heisenberg, they somehow or other *create* the world (or at least the micro-world).

This view is reflected in the mathematical formalism of quantum mechanics. Measurement outcomes – ways the world could be – correspond to the basis vectors (eigenvectors) $|a_1\rangle$, $|a_2\rangle$, . . . of a so-called Hilbert space, a possibly infinite dimensional vector space. (More strictly, an 'observable', which is a property such as momentum, will have a complete set of eigenvectors and eigenvalues associated with it, whereas 'position' which is an incompatible property, will be associated with a different, incompatible set.) But the state of the system $|\psi\rangle$ need not correspond to any one of these base states; instead it might be a superposition of several of them (Figure 5).

In a nutshell, realists are tempted to say reality is one way or another and that superpositions merely reflect our ignorance. Anti-realists deny this; they hold that the micro-world is indeterminate until measurement puts the world into one of the base states.

The anti-realism of the Copenhagen interpretation was met head-on by the beautiful thought experiment dreamed up by Einstein, Podolsky and Rosen (1935), now commonly known as EPR. The argument proceeds by first characterizing some key notions.

Completeness A theory is complete if and only if every element of reality has a counterpart in the theory. Thus, if an electron, for example, has both a position and a momentum, but the theory assigns a value only to one and not the other, then that theory is incomplete.

Criterion of Reality If, without disturbing the system, we can predict with probability one the value of a physical magnitude, then there is an element of reality corresponding to the magnitude. The qualification, 'without disturbing the system', is central. The Copenhagen interpretation holds that measurements do disturb the system, so ascribing an independent reality to any magnitude cannot be based on a (direct and possibly disturbing) measurement.

Locality Two events which are space-like separated (i.e. outside each other's light cones) have no causal influence on one another. They are independent events. This follows from special relativity which holds that nothing, including causal connections, travels faster than light.

The more perspicuous Bohm version of the EPR argument starts with a system, such as an energetic particle, which decays into a pair of photons; these travel in opposite directions along the z axis. Ignoring all but polarization, each photon, call them L and R (for left and right), is associated with its own two-dimensional Hilbert space. The polarization or spin eigenstates will be along any pair of orthogonal axes, say, x and y, or x' and y'. In any given direction a measurement (which yields only eigenvalues) will result in either $+1$ for the spin up state or -1 for the spin down state. We can represent these as $|+\rangle_L$ and $|-\rangle_L$ respectively, for the L photon, and $|+\rangle_R$ and $|-\rangle_R$ for the R photon.

The spin of the system is zero to start with and this must be conserved in the process. Thus, if L has spin magnitude $+1$ in the x direction then R must have -1 in the same direction to keep the total equal to zero. A composite system such as this, in the so-called singlet state, is represented by the equation

$$|\psi\rangle_{LR} = \frac{1}{\sqrt{2}} \left(|+\rangle_L \otimes |-\rangle_R + |-\rangle_L \otimes |+\rangle_R \right)$$

If we measure the spin of the L photon we then know the state of R since the measurement of $|\psi\rangle_{LR}$ immediately puts the whole system into one or other of the two eigenstates. Suppose our measurement resulted in L being polarized in the x direction; i.e. L has spin up in the x direction. This means the state of the whole system is $|+\rangle_L \otimes |-\rangle_R$, from which it follows that the remote photon is in state $|-\rangle_R$; i.e. R has spin down in the x direction. (Choosing the x direction is wholly arbitrary; any other direction could have been measured.) While it might be conceded that the measurement on L may have 'disturbed' it (so it may have created rather than discovered the measurement result), the same cannot be said of R which should be unaffected by our actions. We (at the left wing of the apparatus (Figure 6)) are able to predict with complete certainty the outcome of the measurement on the R photon, and since (by the locality principle) we could not have influenced it in any way with a measurement of L, it follows (by the criterion of reality) that the R magnitude exists independently of measurement. Since this is not reflected in $|\psi\rangle$, it follows (by the criterion of completeness) that QM does not completely describe the whole of reality. EPR then concludes that the theory must be supplemented with local hidden variables in order to give a full description. A local hidden variable is nothing but a factor in the source that is causally responsible for the outcomes at L and R; it is the common cause.

Let us now look at this argument through the eyes of causal empiricism. In the case of the spin state of the near photon, L, our knowledge is based on observation, on direct sensory experience. Our knowing that L has spin up is relatively unproblematic and can be fully accounted for in terms of causal empiricism. But we also immediately know that the remote photon, R, has spin down. How is this knowledge possible? We cannot have any sort of direct observation of R, since it is outside of our light cone. However, if (and this a crucial *if*) there is something at the source which is causally responsible both for the spin state of L and for the spin state of R, then we can be causally connected to R via this common cause in the past of both L and R. Thus, our knowledge of R would be analogous to

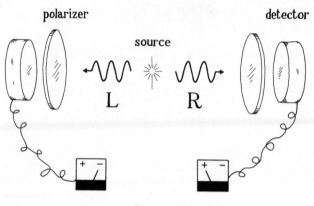

polarizer

source

detector

L   R

Figure 6

our knowledge of the future. Put another way, since we do have knowledge of R, causal empiricism requires that there be something in the common past of L and R which causally grounds our knowledge.

Compelling though EPR is, it cannot be right. This is the upshot of several related findings known collectively as the Bell results. Bell's original derivation of an inequality which bears his name was rather complicated, but versions are now so simple that it would be a shame to pass it by. I shall begin with a simple derivation of a Bell-type inequality, and then briefly describe its experimental refutation.

Let us start by considering an EPR-type set-up. Unlike EPR, however, we will consider measurements of spin in different directions, say, along a and a' for the L photon and b and b' for the R photon. There are four possible pairs of measurements that could be made:

$$(a, b) \quad (a', b) \quad (a, b') \quad (a', b')$$

where (a, b) means the L photon is measured for spin along the a axis and R along the b axis. A spin up result of a measurement has value $+1$, and spin down -1. Now define a correlation function $c(x, y)$ as follows.

If $a = 1$ and $b = 1$, then $c(a, b) = 1 \times 1 = 1$;
if $a = 1$ and $b = -1$, then $c(a, b) = 1 \times -1 = -1$;

and so on for a', b' etc. (where $a = 1$ means that the result

106

of measuring the L photon in the **a** direction is +1 etc. Note that **a** is the direction of measurement and a is the result).

We imagine running the experiment many times. After N tests, with a_i being the ith result, we have the generalized correlation function defined as

$$c(\mathbf{a},\ \mathbf{b}) = \frac{1}{N} \Sigma_i a_i b_i$$

We will now make two key assumptions.

Realism   Each photon has all of its properties all of the time; in particular, each has a spin up or spin down magnitude in every direction whether there is a spin measurement made in that direction or not.

This assumption is embedded in the mathematics as follows. Let a_i (or a'_i, b_i, b'_i) be the result of the ith measurement, if made in the **a** (or **a'**, **b**, **b'**, respectively) direction. The value is either +1 or −1 and this value exists whether the measurement is made or not. In particular, if photon L is measured in the **a** direction then it cannot be measured in the **a'** direction; nevertheless, even though we cannot know what it is, we still assume that it has one value or the other. This is the core of realism – measurements do not create, they discover what is independently there.

Locality   The results of measurement on one side of the apparatus do not depend on what is happening at the other side. The outcome of a spin measurement on photon L is independent of the *direction* in which R is measured (i.e. the orientation of the apparatus), and is even independent of whether R is measured at all.

Formally, the locality assumption is captured by having the value a_i independent of the values b_i and b'_i. So if a measurement of L in the **a** direction would result in +1 if R were measured in the **b** direction, it would still be +1 if R were measured in the **b'** direction instead.

Now consider the following expression:

$$a_i b_i + a_i b'_i + a'_i b_i - a'_i b'_i.$$

Rearranging terms we have

$$a_i(b_i + b'_i) + a'_i(b_i - b'_i).$$

Since the a terms equal $+1$ or -1, and since one of the terms in parentheses equals 0 while the other equals either $+2$ or -2, the value of the whole expression is $+2$ or -2. Taking the absolute value, we have

$$\left| a_i b_i + a_i b'_i + a'_i b_i - a'_i b'_i \right| = 2.$$

This holds for the ith measurement result. The generalization for N measurements is therefore

$$\left| \frac{1}{N} \Sigma_i \, a_i b_i + a_i b'_i + a'_i b_i - a'_i b'_i \right| \leq 2.$$

In terms of the correlation function we have

$$\left| c\left(a, \, b\right) + c(a, \, b') + c(a', \, b) - c(a', \, b') \right| \leq 2.$$

This is a simple form of Bell's inequality. It means that when spin measurements are done for arbitrary directions a and a' on the L photons and b and b' on the R photons, we can expect that degree of correlation.

It is important to stress that the inequality is derived by a simple combinatorial argument based on two common-sense assumptions: realism and locality. After many tests the correlation between the L and R photons, taken a pair at a time, must satisfy this inequality – if the assumptions of realism and locality both hold.

QM, however, makes a different prediction. An experimental test pitting QM against Local Realism, as it is often called, is thus possible. Amazingly, a metaphysical theory has empirical consequences.

To get specific QM predictions we need to specify directions in which the spin measurements are to be made. Let $a = b$, otherwise the orientations of a and b can be arbitrary; furthermore, let a' be $-45°$ and b' be $+45°$ from the common a/b direction (Figure 7).

According to QM the correlation functions have the following values:

$$c\left(a, \, b\right) \ = - \cos 0 = -1$$
$$c\left(a, \, b'\right) \ = - \cos 45 = -1/\sqrt{2}$$
$$c\left(a', \, b\right) \ = - \cos 45 = -1/\sqrt{2}$$
$$c\left(a', \, b'\right) \ = - \cos 90 = 0.$$

What this means is that if (in the first of the four cases), L is

different orientations of
measuring apparatus

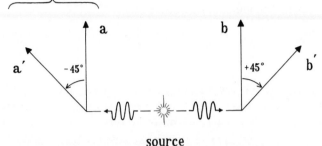

source

Figure 7

measured in the *a* direction and has, say spin up, then R measured in the *b* (= *a*) direction will not have spin up. They are perfectly negatively correlated. In the fourth case when L and R are measured at right angles to each other the results of measurement are completely uncorrelated. The other two cases yield results in between.

We now substitute these values, derived from QM for these same angles, into the Bell inequality:

$$\left|- 1 - \frac{1}{\sqrt{2}} - \frac{1}{\sqrt{2}} - 0\right| = 1 + \frac{2}{\sqrt{2}} > 2.$$

Thus, at these angles, QM and Local Realism diverge in their predictions, making an empirical test possible of what previously was thought to be pure speculative metaphysics. There have been several tests of the inequality and in almost every one QM has made the right predictions, Local Realism the wrong ones. Of all these tests, the ones carried out by Aspect *et al.*[5] have been the most sophisticated.

The crucial feature of the Aspect experiment is the presence of very fast optical switches which direct L photons to either *a* or *a'* and R photons to either *b* or *b'* measurements. They each pick a direction randomly, while the photons are in flight. The reason this is considered important is that in earlier experiments the setting of the distant measuring device was fixed long before the measurement, thus allowing the possibility of a subluminal signal between the distant wings of the apparatus and, hence, the possibility that they could 'communicate' with one another. Of course, that may seem bizarre, but the QM world is so weird that it is always nice to have one more possibility ruled out, however farfetched it may seem.

THE UPSHOT

Here's the moral for causal empiricism: *it won't work.* Our knowledge of the measurement result at the far wing of the apparatus cannot be based upon any sort of causal connection with that outcome. First, it cannot be directly connected, since that would violate special relativity; and second, it cannot be indirectly connected via a common cause in the past either, since that would amount to local hidden variables, the very thing ruled out by the Bell results. Consequently, we have knowledge of some part of the physical world which is not the result of any physically causal sensory process.

At this point readers may object and voice the obvious reply which comes to mind: our knowledge of the remote outcome is due to a theory-based calculation that we can easily make. We have directly measured, say, spin up on our side, and we know the theory, i.e. total spin is conserved; so we conclude that the remote outcome must be spin down. We do this sort of inferring all the time, as for instance when we know two things from experience which serve as premises ('It is raining' and 'If it is raining then the ground is wet') and we deduce a third from these premises ('The ground is wet'). We needn't inspect the ground directly to know this, yet we still know it from experience. Isn't our knowledge of the remote outcome in the EPR set-up just like that?

Alas, it is not. Consider the conditional sentence, 'If it is raining then the ground is wet'. It is really a kind of generalization, a mini-law of nature; so let us call it our theory. (It is analogous to the quantum mechanical theory about spin conservation which allows us to draw the inference about the remote outcome.) But what is the relation of my belief in this theory to particular bits of rained upon wet ground? That is, what is my relation to the theory's instances? If my (presumably true) belief in the theory is appropriately *causally connected to each and every instance* of wet ground (perhaps they are linked via the Big

110

Bang), then causal empiricism is saved (at least in the wet ground case). But this makes the wet ground example completely unlike the EPR case, since there is no such causal connection in the latter. My belief in spin conservation is not causally connected to the physically remote spinning photon – not even via the Big Bang. On the other hand, if my belief in the rain-makes-the-ground-wet theory is not causally connected – somehow or other – to all the particular wet grounds, then the two cases are similar, but causal empiricism is equally wrong in both. Generalizations have always been problematic for causal theories of knowledge.

Ignoring 'my belief in the theory' and instead focusing on the theory itself, we can raise similar problems. First, if a theory is an abstract entity, then it can only be in causal contact with the remote photon in some sense of 'causal contact' that no normal empiricist would allow. And second, if the theory is my token of the theory (e.g. the physical textbook I carry to my wing of the measuring apparatus and use when making calculations), then by the Bell results the theory is definitely not in causal contact with the remote photon. (Contrast this with the fact that I come into causal contact with Moses just by looking at the printed word 'Moses' in my copy of the Old Testament, since there is a causal chain leading from Moses to the printing of his name.)

At this point one might say that at best the argument shows that the *causal* ingredient in causal empiricism is wrong, not that we have a priori knowledge. Perhaps we have been too rigid in characterizing knowledge. A priori knowledge could come about by violating either the sense-experience condition or the causal condition. Maybe we should abandon the latter. After all, the causal theory is a rather recent addition to the empiricist outlook; it is not at all a part of the tradition handed down from Locke, Berkeley, Hume, Mill and the positivists, and so can easily be jettisoned.

However, it is not so easy to concede this point. Traditional empiricists only claimed knowledge of sense-data, while typical contemporary empiricists want knowledge of the world. The causal ingredient seems a necessary and plausible link between sense-experience and the world that we try to get a grip on. Moreover, Gettier-type counter-examples to the traditional analysis of knowledge have been met by including a causal ingredient: the knower must not only have true justified belief, but must be causally connected to the object of knowledge, as well.[6] To abandon the causal component in contemporary empiricism is to allow a large class of problems back into the fold. A different route is preferable, one with a significant liberalization of the notion of cause.

The causes in the causal theory of knowledge have always been thought of as efficient causes of a completely physical sort. (Photons come from the tea cup, interact with the rods and cones in the eye etc.) Let us expand the causal theory of knowledge to include the causal powers of abstract objects. Thus, we will suppose there are abstract objects – numbers, values, properties, laws of nature – and that these things causally interact with us, though not in any sort of physical way. Following Gödel, we can say that (in some special cases) we 'perceive' these independently existing abstract objects just as surely as we perceive tea cups. This sort of perception – often called intuition – has much in common with ordinary experience; but since it does not involve the ordinary physical senses, any knowledge deriving from it is justly called a priori. Let us so baptize them: if knowledge is based on sensory experience involving a physical causal connection, then it is a posteriori; if it involves an abstract causal connection by-passing the physical senses, then it is a priori.

But we still want to understand how it is possible to know the remote measurement result in an EPR-type experiment. Given that there is no physical causal connection from the remote spin state to ourselves at one wing of the apparatus, how do we come to know about the result at the other wing?

THE ARGUMENT SO FAR

Before getting into thought experiments, it might be a good idea to summarize things to this point. Here's what I hope to have established.

1 Laws of nature are relations between properties; they are abstract entities, outside of space and time; they exist independently of us; and they are somehow or other responsible for the events of the physical world.

2 The causal theory of knowledge does not stand in the way of

this theory; we can have knowledge of X without being causally connected to X.

3 We have a priori knowledge in the case of an EPR set-up. The best explanation for how this might be is through the assumption that in such a situation we grasp the relevant law of nature.

4 Most of our knowledge of laws of nature is based on normal empirical evidence; we causally interact with instances of the law, not with the abstract entities themselves. But the EPR situation gives us hope of a more direct contact, an immediate connection, a seeing into Plato's heaven with 'the mind's eye'.

The next section takes up this last point and tries to establish the following.

5 Some thought experiments allow us to 'see' the laws of nature. This direct grasp of the abstract realm yields a priori knowledge of the physical world, a view which hasn't been taken seriously since the seventeenth century, which is rightly known as the 'century of genius'.

THOUGHT EXPERIMENTS

I won't try to define thought experiments, but simply note that we recognize them when we see them: they are visualizable; they involve mental manipulations; they are not the mere consequence of a theory-based calculation; they are often (but not always) impossible to implement as real experiments, either because we lack the relevant technology or because they are simply impossible in principle. What I would like to do now is look at the finest example of a thought experiment of which I know: Galileo's wonderful argument in the *Discoursi* to show that all bodies, regardless of their weight, fall at the same speed (*Discoursi*, 66f.). It begins by noting Aristotle's view that heavier bodies fall faster than light ones ($H > L$). We are then asked to imagine that a heavy cannon ball is attached to a light musket ball. What would happen if they were released together (Figure 8)?

Reasoning in the Aristotelian manner leads to an absurd conclusion. First, the light ball will slow up the heavy one (acting as a kind of drag), so the speed of the combined system will be slower than the speed of the heavy ball falling alone

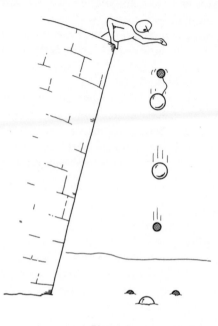

Figure 8

($H > H + L$). On the other hand, the combined system is heavier than the heavy ball alone, so it should fall faster ($H + L > H$). We now have the absurd consequence that the heavy ball is both faster and slower than the even heavier combined system. Thus, the Aristotelian theory of falling bodies is destroyed.

But the question remains, 'Which falls faster?' The right answer is now plain as day. The paradox is resolved by making them equal; they all fall at the same speed ($H = L = H + L$).

Galileo's thought experiment is quite remarkable. Though such reasoning is fallible, it is not a piece of standard, empirical, conjectural, a posteriori knowledge. Rather, we are justified in calling this a case of a priori science. Here's why. First, *there have been no new empirical data*. I suppose this is almost true by definition; being a *thought* experiment rules out new empirical input. It is not that there are no empirical data involved in the thought experiment at all. The emphasis is on *new* sensory input; it is this that is lacking in the thought experiment. What we are trying to explain is the *transition* from the old to the new theory and that is not readily explained in terms of empirical input unless there is new empirical input.

Second, *Galileo's new theory is not logically deduced from old data. Nor is it any kind of logical truth.* A second way of making new discoveries – a way which does not trouble empiricists – is by deducing them from old data. Perhaps Galileo's thought experiment is really an argument. Is this plausible? I think not. The premises of such an argument could include all the data that went into Aristotle's theory. From this Galileo derived a contradiction. (So far, so good; we have a straightforward argument to this point.) But can we derive Galileo's theory that all bodies fall at the same rate from these same premises? Well, in one sense, yes, since we can derive anything from a contradiction; but this hardly seems fair.[7] What's more, whatever we can derive from these premises is immediately questionable since, on the basis of the contradiction, we now rightly consider our belief in the premises to be undermined.

Might Galileo's theory be true by logic alone? To see that the theory that all bodies fall at the same rate is not a logical truth, it suffices to note that bodies might fall with different speeds depending on their colours or on their chemical composition as has recently been claimed.[8] These considerations undermine the argument view of thought experiments.

Third, *the transition from Aristotle's to Galileo's theory is not just a case of making the simplest overall adjustment to the old theory.* It may well be the case that the transition was the simplest, but that was not the reason for making it. (I doubt that simplicity or other aesthetic considerations ever play a useful role in science, but for the sake of the argument, let's allow that they could.) Suppose the degree of rational belief in Aristotle's theory of falling bodies is r, where $0 < r < 1$. After the thought experiment has been performed and the new theory adopted, the degree of rational belief in Galileo's theory is r', where $0 < r < r' < 1$. That is, I make the historical claim that the degree of rational belief in Galileo's theory was *higher* just after the thought experiment than it was in Aristotle's just before. (Note the times of appraisal here. Obviously the degree of rational belief in Aristotle's theory *after* the contradiction is found approaches zero.) Appeals to the notion of smallest belief revision won't even begin to explain this fact. We have not just a new theory – we have a better one.

Let me conclude by briefly contrasting this form of apriorism about physics with earlier forms of rationalism. Unlike Plato, Descartes or Leibniz etc., a priori knowledge on my view is neither certain nor innate. It is not put there by God; it is not recollected; nor is it infallible. But like the traditional rationalists, I hold that there is an abstract realm which is perfectly real and that we can know much about it.

7

PHENOMENA

PHENOMENA AND DATA

Phenomena! Now there's a word to conjure with. It is what our theories try to explain, and what we use to justify those theories. It is what instrumentalists try to save, and what realists try to get beyond. It is what Ian Hacking thinks we create in the laboratory (in contrast to nature) and what Kant took to be partly the work of the mind (in contrast to noumena).

My point of departure is a notable recent analysis of phenomena by James Bogen and James Woodward who make a 'distinction between phenomena and data' (1988, 305). The former are constructed[1] out of the later.

> Data, which play the role of evidence for the existence of phenomena, for the most part can be straightforwardly observed. However, data typically cannot be predicted or systematically explained by theory. By contrast, well-developed scientific theories do predict and explain facts about phenomena. Phenomena are detected through the use of data, but in most cases are not observable in any interesting sense of that term.
>
> (1988, 305)

> Data are . . . idiosyncratic to particular experimental contexts, and typically cannot occur outside of those contexts. . . . Phenomena, by contrast, are not idiosyncratic to specific experimental contexts. We expect phenomena to have stable, repeatable characteristics which will be detect-

117

able by means of a variety of different procedures, which may yield quite different kinds of data.

(1988, 317)

There are several important features and consequences of this view. Among the more important are these: explanation is not a relation between theories and observable facts; nor is prediction; theories are not tested by comparing them with experience; and observation – whether theory-laden or not – is 'much less central to understanding science than many have supposed' (1988, 305).

Typical of Bogen–Woodward phenomena are weak neutral currents. The associated data are bubble chamber photographs. The relevant theory which is supported by all of this is the Weinberg–Salam theory of weak interactions. It is supported, not by the data, but by the phenomena of weak neutral currents. The existence of the phenomena is in turn supported by the data, the photographs. According to Bogen and Woodward, the data are far too messy to serve as evidence for any theory; the phenomena play a crucial and irreducible intermediate role in the process of scientific inference. (For further discussions, rich with examples, see Woodward 1989, Harper 1990 and Kaiser 1991.)

It is worth noting that the distinction (or something like it) enjoys a wonderful historical precedent. In his *Principia* Newton claimed to 'deduce' the theory of universal gravitation 'from the phenomena'. What he had in mind as phenomena were Kepler's laws. Quite understandably, historians have often balked at Newton's claim, preferring to see his effort as a case of making a bold hypothesis which turned out to be wonderfully confirmed by experience. But if we take Newton's 'phenomena' to mean something constructed out of the data of experience, then Newton's claim is interestingly plausible.

There has been a sustained tradition in the philosophy of science of distinguishing between (i) deep explanatory theories, (ii) phenomena and phenomenological laws and (iii) empirical data. William Whewell, for example, thought inferences from empirical data were of distinct sorts:

> Inductive truths are of two kinds, Laws of Phenomena, and Theories of Causes. It is necessary to begin every science with the Laws of Phenomena; but it is impossible

that we should be satisfied to stop short of a Theory of Causes.

(1858, Aphorism xxiv)

Whewell held an interesting blend of views stemming from Kant and Plato. He was the antithesis of the latter-day positivist, Ernest Nagel. Nevertheless, the two were like-minded on this matter; both saw science as having these three distinct components. After noting that 'Scientific thought takes its ultimate point of departure from problems suggested by observing things and events encountered in common experience' (1961, 79), Nagel goes on to distinguish between empirical generalizations and theories:

> Let us baptize the *prima facie* difference between laws just noted by calling those of the first sort 'experimental laws' and those of the second sort 'theoretical laws' (or simply 'theories'). In consonance with this terminological stipulation and the distinction covered by it, the law that the pressure of an ideal gas whose temperature is constant varies inversely with its volume . . . [is] classified as an experimental law. . . . On the other hand, the set of assumptions asserting different chemical elements to be composed of different kinds of atoms which remain undivided in chemical transformations . . . [is] classified as [a theory].

(1961, 80)

Nancy Cartwright's view of science is far removed from either Whewell's or Nagel's, but she still maintains a threefold division among singular events, phenomenological laws and fundamental or theoretical laws.

> For the physicist, unlike the philosopher, the distinction between theoretical and phenomenological has nothing to do with what is observable and what is unobservable. Instead the terms separate laws which are fundamental and explanatory from those that merely describe.

(1983, 2)

Obviously, the distinctions made by Whewell, Nagel and Cartwright are not exactly the same. Nor are they the same as those, following Bogen and Woodward, that I want to urge. Nagel's empirical laws, for example, consist of observation

119

terms only, while Cartwright's phenomenological theories may contain all sorts of theoretical concepts. And Whewell is a realist about the deep explanatory laws of science while the other two are not. But there is enough similarity of motivation and doctrine to make lumping them together instructive, if not wholly accurate. Though the distinctions I want to argue for will not be precisely the same as any of Whewell's, Nagel's or Cartwright's, the crucial main point is that there are distinctions among theories, phenomena and data.

To illustrate the phenomena/data distinction in some detail, let us look at the example of Joule and the mechanical equivalent of heat. In the middle of the nineteenth century James Joule established the mechanical equivalent of heat, i.e. he showed 'That the quantity of heat produced by friction of bodies, whether solid or liquid, is always proportional to the quantity of force expended'. As well as a general equivalence, Joule concluded quite specifically on the basis of his experiments:

> That the quantity of heat capable of increasing the temperature of a pound of water (weighed in vacuo, and taken at between 55° and 60°) by 1°F, requires for its evolution the expenditure of a mechanical force represented by the fall of 772 lbs through the space of one foot.
>
> (1850, 82)

This is a phenomenon, not a datum of experience. How did Joule get it? He constructed a paddle wheel device which produced a great deal of friction in a container of water. The paddles were driven by a system of weights and pulleys (Figure 9).

> The method of experimenting was simply as follows: The temperature of the frictional apparatus having been ascertained and the weights wound up . . . the roller was refixed to the axis. The precise height of the weights above the ground having then been determined by means of the graduated slips of wood . . . the roller was set at liberty and allowed to revolve until the weights reached the flagged floor of the laboratory, after accomplishing a fall of about 63 inches. The roller was then removed to the stand, the weights wound up again, and the friction renewed. After this had been repeated twenty times, the experi-

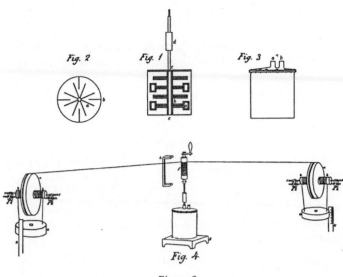

Figure 9

ment was concluded with another observation of the temperature of the apparatus. The mean temperature of the laboratory was determined by observations made at the commencement, middle and termination of each experiment.

(Joule, 1850, 66)

Joule took great care to minimize the effects of radiant heat: by insulating the container, by having a wooden barrier between the apparatus and the experimenter, and so on. Nevertheless, heat radiation figured in all his calculations:

Previously to, or immediately after each of the experiments, I made trial of the effect of radiation and conduction of heat to or from the atmosphere, in depressing or raising the temperature of the frictional apparatus. In these trials, the position of the apparatus, the quantity of water contained by it, the time occupied, the method of observing the thermometers, the position of the experimenter, in short everything, with the exception of the apparatus being at rest, was the same as in the experiments in which the effect of friction was observed.

(1850, 66)

Table 2 gives Joule's results (i.e. data). Joule calculated the role of radiation as follows:

> From the various experiments in the above table [Table 2] in which the effect of radiation was observed, it may be readily gathered that the effect of the temperature of the surrounding air upon the apparatus was, for each degree of difference between the mean temperature of the air and that of the apparatus, 0.04654°. Therefore, since the excess of the temperature of the atmosphere over that of the apparatus was 0.32295° in the mean of the radiation experiments, but only 0.305075° in the mean of the friction experiments, it follows that 0.000832° must be added to the difference between 0.57525° and 0.012975°, and the result, 0.563107°, will be the proximate heating effect of the friction.

Joule continues:

> But to this quantity a small correction must be applied on account of the mean of the temperatures of the apparatus at the commencement and the termination of each friction experiment having been taken for the true mean temperature, which was not strictly the case, owing to the somewhat less rapid increase of temperature towards the termination of the experiment when the water had become warmer. The mean temperature of the apparatus in the friction experiments ought therefore to be estimated 0.002184° higher, which will diminish the heating effect of the atmosphere by 0.000102°. This, added to 0.563107°, gives 0.563209° as the true mean increase of temperature due to the friction of water.

But this is far from the end of it.

> In order to ascertain the absolute quantity of heat evolved, it was necessary to find the capacity for heat of the copper vessel and brass paddle wheel. . . .
>
> (1850, 69)

Joule proceeds to calculate the specific heat of the various components of the apparatus, including a brass stopper, the thermometers which did the measuring and so on. And then there was the energy lost (in the form of heat produced) due to friction

Table 2

Number of experiment and cause of change of temperature	Total fall of weights in inches	Mean temperature of air	Difference between mean of columns 5 and 6 and column 3	Temperature of apparatus		Gain or loss of heat during experiment
				Commencement of experiment	Termination of experiment	
1 Friction	1256.96	57.698°	−2.252°	55.118°	55.774°	0.656° gain
1 Radiation	0	57.868	−2.040	55.774	55.882	0.108 gain
2 Friction	1255.16	58.085	−1.875	55.882	56.539	0.657 gain
2 Radiation	0	58.370	−1.789	56.539	56.624	0.085 gain
3 Friction	1253.66	60.788	−1.596	58.870	59.515	0.645 gain
3 Radiation	0	60.926	−1.373	59.515	59.592	0.077 gain
4 Friction	1252.74	61.001	−1.110	59.592	60.191	0.599 gain
4 Radiation	0	60.890	−0.684	60.191	60.222	0.031 gain
5 Friction	1251.81	60.940	−0.431	60.222	60.797	0.575 gain
5 Radiation	0	61.035	−0.237	60.797	60.799	0.002 gain
6 Radiation	0	59.675	+0.125	59.805	59.795	0.010 loss
6 Friction	1254.71	59.919	+0.157	59.795	60.357	0.562 gain
7 Radiation	0	59.888	−0.209	59.677	59.681	0.004 gain
7 Friction	1254.02	60.076	−0.111	59.681	60.249	0.568 gain
8 Radiation	0	58.240	+0.609	58.871	58.828	0.043 loss
8 Friction	1251.22	58.237	+0.842	58.828	59.330	0.502 gain
9 Friction	1253.92	55.328	+0.070	55.118	55.678	0.560 gain
9 Radiation	0	55.528	+0.148	55.678	53.674	0.004 loss
10 Radiation	0	54.941	−0.324	54.614	54.620	0.006 gain
10 Friction	1257.96	54.985	−0.835	54.620	55.180	0.560 gain
11 Radiation	0	55.111	+0.069	55.180	55.180	0.000
11 Friction	1258.59	55.229	+0.227	55.180	55.733	0.553 gain
12 Friction	1258.71	55.433	+0.238	55.388	55.954	0.566 gain
12 Radiation	0	55.687	+0.265	55.954	55.950	0.004 loss
13 Friction	1257.91	55.677	+0.542	55.950	56.488	0.538 gain
13 Radiation	0	55.674	+0.800	56.488	56.461	0.027 loss
14 Radiation	0	55.579	−0.583	54.987	55.006	0.019 gain
14 Friction	1259.69	55.864	−0.568	55.006	55.587	0.581 gain
15 Radiation	0	56.047	−0.448	55.587	55.612	0.025 gain
15 Friction	1259.89	56.182	−0.279	55.612	56.195	0.583 gain
16 Friction	1259.64	55.368	+0.099	55.195	55.739	0.544 gain
16 Radiation	0	55.483	+0.250	55.739	55.728	0.011 loss
17 Friction	1259.64	55.498	+0.499	55.728	56.266	0.538 gain
17 Radiation	0	55.541	+0.709	56.266	56.235	0.031 loss
18 Radiation	0	56.769	−1.512	55.230	55.284	0.054 gain
18 Friction	1260.17	56.966	−1.372	55.284	55.905	0.621 gain
19 Radiation	0	60.058	−1.763	58.257	58.334	0.077 gain
19 Friction	1262.24	60.112	−1.450	58.334	58.990	0.656 gain
20 Radiation	0	60.567	−1.542	58.990	59.060	0.070 gain
20 Friction	1261.94	60.611	−1.239	59.060	59.685	0.625 gain
21 Friction	1264.07	58.654	−0.321	58.050	58.616	0.566 gain
21 Radiation	0	58.627	−0.018	58.616	58.603	0.013 loss
22 Friction	1262.97	58.631	+0.243	58.603	59.145	0.542 gain
22 Radiation	0	58.624	+0.505	59.145	59.114	0.031 loss
23 Friction	1264.72	59.689	−1.100	58.284	58.894	0.610 gain
23 Radiation	0	59.943	−1.027	58.894	58.938	0.044 gain

in the pulleys, and many other considerations besides. All of these must figure in his final calculations.

Table 3

Number of series	Material employed	Equivalent in air	Equivalent in vacuo	Mean
1	Water	773.640	772.692	772.692
2	Mercury	773.762	772.814	} 774.083
3	Mercury	776.303	775.352	
4	Cast iron	776.997	776.045	} 774.987
5	Cast iron	774.880	773.930	

The experiment was run in a variety of circumstances, and the results Joule summarized as in Table 3. He then remarked,

> I consider that 772.692, the equivalent derived from the friction of water, is the most correct, both on account of the number of experiments tried, and the great capacity of the apparatus for heat. And since, even in the friction of fluids, it was impossible entirely to avoid vibration and the production of a slight sound, it is probable that the above number is slightly in excess.
>
> (1850, 82)

Out of this great mass of experimental data, calculation and educated conjecture comes Joule's final opinion (which I quote again):

> That the quantity of heat produced by the friction of bodies, whether solid or liquid, is always proportional to the quantity of force expended. And that the quantity of heat capable of increasing the temperature of a pound of water (weighed in vacuo, and taken at between 55° and 60°) by 1°F, requires for its evolution the expenditure of a mechanical force represented by the fall of 772 lbs through the space of one foot.
>
> (1850, 82)

Thus is a phenomenon born.

PHENOMENA AND NATURAL KINDS

The world is full of data, but there are relatively few phenomena. My suggestion is rather simple: *phenomena are abstract entities which are (or at least correspond to) visualizable natural kinds.* When scientists construct the phenomena out of a great mass of data what they are doing is singling out what they take to be genuine natural kinds. In Plato's gruesome metaphor, they are trying to cut nature at its joints. To this I would only add: at nature's visualizable joints.

Everybody's paradigm of a natural kind is a chemical element. The Periodic Table is a classification scheme of the elements in accordance with their essential properties. It is also a paradigm of the construction of phenomena out of data. The phenomena are represented by the entries in the table – the chemical elements and their properties: atomic weights, atomic numbers, chemical similarities etc.

There is no algorithm for making phenomena out of data – it is a fallible process. Pinning down natural kinds and their essential properties is no easy matter, as the history of the Periodic Table well illustrates. Demitri Mendeléev ordered the elements according to their increasing atomic weights. But he noticed that atoms with similar chemical properties recurred periodically at fairly regular intervals. By lumping together those which are chemically similar he created a classification of the elements known as the Periodic Table.

Though brilliantly conceived, Mendeléev's taxonomy was somewhat problematic. In the case of a few elements, ordering them by increasing weight was at odds with ordering them in accord with their chemical properties. And the discovery of isotopes (which have different weights but are chemically identical) made matters even worse. This was the background for Henry Mosely's work, begun in 1913.

The characteristic frequencies associated with each of the elements is due, according to Bohr's theory of the atom, to electrons in orbit around the nucleus falling to lower orbits. When they fall from one energy level, or shell, to a lower one they emit a photon of the appropriate energy, or frequency.

Mosely fired cathode rays at several of the heavier elements and recorded the X-ray frequencies produced. He focused on a particular series known as the K_α-lines in a large number of elements. What he discovered is that as the atomic number increases by 1 (i.e., as $Z \to Z + 1$), the quantity $(4/3 \times \nu(Z) \times R)^{1/2}$ also increases by 1. This led to the following formula for the frequencies of K_α-series for the element with atomic number Z: $\nu(Z) = (Z - 1)^2 \times (1/1^2 - 1/2^2) \times R$. R is the Rydberg constant, known independently, and $1/1^2 - 1/2^2$ is associated with the first and second energy levels. See Figure 10 and Table 4.

Mosely's classification and Mendeléev's coincide except in a few cases. For example, potassium preceded argon in Mendeléev's table, but Mosely reversed them. This resulted in Mosely's Periodic Table being in full agreement with both the recurring regularities of the chemical properties and the increasing atomic numbers. There is no internal tension as there was in Mendeléev's taxonomy.

The shift in the ordering structure of the Periodic Table, from atomic weights to atomic numbers, shows the complexity and ingenuity that is sometimes involved in constructing phenomena out of data. But it also shows the importance of natural kinds and their essential properties in scientific thinking. Mosely expressed it well when he summed up his experimental work.

> We have here a proof that there is in the atom a fundamental quantity, which increases by regular steps as we pass from one element to the next. This quantity can only be the charge on the central nucleus, of the existence of which we already have definite proof.
>
> (Quoted in Trigg 1975, 32f.)

Notice that Mosely is not claiming to have discovered that the nucleus has a charge, any more than he is denying that the elements have an atomic weight. His claim is about which of these existing properties is 'fundamental', or essential (chemically), and which is not.

In passing, it should be noted that the history of the Periodic Table provides another argument for distinguishing phenomena from data. When the table was first created there were 'gaps'; i.e. nothing had ever been observed which corresponded to certain places in the table. Any theory (such as Bohr's) that attempted to explain the features of the table would be required to account for every place in the table, including the gaps. (Or explain why the gaps had to exist, as quantum mechanics does

Wave Length × 10⁴cms

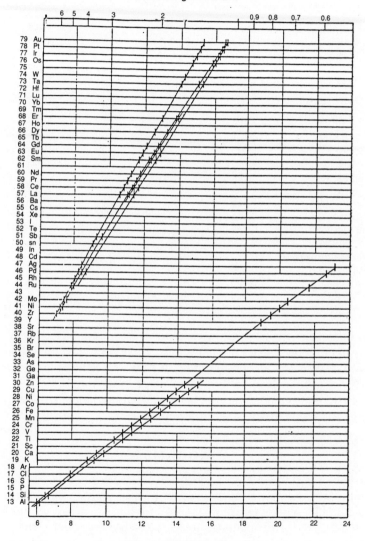

Square root of frequency × 10⁻⁶

Figure 10

127

Table 4

	α line $\lambda \times 10^8$ cm	Q_K	N Atomic number	β line $\lambda \times 10^8$ cm
Aluminium	8.364	12.05	13	7.912
Silicon	7.142	13.04	14	6.729
Chlorine	4.750	16.00	17	–
Potassium	3.759	17.98	19	3.463
Calcium	3.368	19.00	20	3.094
Titanium	2.758	20.99	22	2.524
Vanadium	2.519	21.96	23	2.297
Chromium	2.301	22.98	24	2.093
Manganese	2.111	23.99	25	1.818
Iron	1.946	24.99	26	1.765
Cobalt	1.798	26.00	27	1.629
Nickel	1.662	27.04	28	1.506
Copper	1.549	28.01	29	1.402
Zinc	1.445	29.01	30	1.306
Yttrium	0.838	38.1	39	–
Zirconium	0.794	39.1	40	–
Niobium	0.750	40.2	41	–
Molybdenum	0.721	41.2	42	–
Ruthenium	0.638	43.6	44	–
Palladium	0.584	45.6	46	–
Silver	0.560	46.6	47	–

in the case of the very heavy elements – they are unstable.) This means that the entries in the Periodic Table cannot be identified with what is actually observed, with data – since there are none – but should instead be thought of as phenomena.

I said that phenomena are *visualizable* natural kinds. Let's turn now to this picturable aspect of phenomena.

DIAGRAMS

Artists' diagrams are another example of phenomena, and an important example at that. Photographs of high energy events in a bubble chamber are instances of data. But we're all quite used to having this material presented to us twice over – first as data (in our strict sense), then as phenomena. Figure 11 gives an example taken from a standard source. There are two obvious but important things to note in examples such as this. First, that there is a world of difference between the chicken scratches on

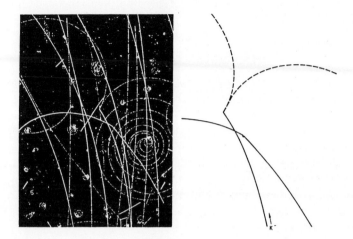

Figure 11

the left and the artist's drawing on the right. And second, that theories explain what is happening on the right; they never try to cope with the mess on the left. This may seem a trivial point – once the distinction is made. Perhaps it is, but the distinction requires treating data and phenomena as profoundly different things.

No one nowadays believes in raw data; observations are always conceptualized. (This is undoubtedly one of the great results of modern philosophy of science, due to Hanson, Kuhn, Feyerabend, Sellars and many others.) Isn't 'phenomena' just another name for this, i.e. for theory-laden data?[2] In many cases the distinction between phenomena and conceptualized or theory-laden data will seem artificial. (High energy physicists like to say they can just see the sub-nuclear process right in the bubble chamber photo.) But there are clear cases which cannot be treated as theory-laden observations. The elements of the Periodic Table are phenomena, and some of them, e.g. Fe (iron), might successfully be treated as observable in some theory-laden way. But there are others, e.g. Ge (germanium), which (at the time of Mendeléev) were simply not seen at all. Similarly, in thought experiments (to be discussed in a moment), phenomena, such as the light bending in Einstein's elevator, are not actually seen, either. These examples of phenomena cannot be reduced to actual observable data, theory-laden or not.

PHENOMENA AND VALUES

E. O. Wilson's *Sociobiology: The New Synthesis* (1975) has been a profoundly influential book. Amazingly, it has almost no photos, but lots and lots of very impressive drawings. This may be no accident. Sociobiology is often charged with offering bogus explanations, i.e. with first mis-describing behaviours and then giving pseudo-Darwinian explanations of these non-facts. If sociobiologists (like other scientists) are actually in the business of explaining phenomena rather than data, then drawings provide a wonderful way of getting 'values' into the evidence.

In one particular drawing we see two dinosaurs struggling with one another (Wilson 1975, 211). They are obviously in some sort of combat. It goes without saying that dinosaur fights have been witnessed by no palaeontologist. The caption only says that as depicted the dinosaurs are agile and not sluggish, but we see so much more than this. We see aggression, a fight for dominance. Another drawing depicts several dolphins; one has been harpooned. Others are grouped around, some trying to push the wounded one to the surface for air (1975, 226). In the drawing we see altruistic behaviour (as the caption indicates), but in the wild when a dolphin is hit by a harpoon observers would only see a lot of blood, thrashing about and the grouping around of other dolphins. The artist's drawing is a visualizable reconstruction of what is happening. Gifted artists can do something no photographer can do – draw emotions, feelings, moods and attitudes. These become part of the phenomena. Sociobiologists then use evolutionary biology to explain the phenomena, the aggression or the altruistic behaviour in the drawings. They do not try to explain the data, neither the dolphins' splashing about that has actually been experienced, nor the dinosaurs' antics, which hasn't.

Londa Schiebinger's *The Mind Has No Sex?* (1989) makes a strong case concerning the value-ladenness of the 'facts' (i.e. phenomena, in the terms used here). Nineteenth-century artists' drawings of male and female skeletons, for example, are a far cry from raw data.

Schiebinger's is one of many excellent feminist books on science that have recently appeared. Like the work of other feminist critics, hers will have a beneficial impact on the practice of science. She is a reformer, unlike Rorty and Latour whose work only culminates in a benign indifference to science. Scheibinger, in particular, is interested in how sexist values get injected into biology. Her study of anatomy texts and illustrations is extremely instructive. A particularly striking example is a pair of diagrams taken from a nineteenth-century text. A male skeleton is depicted along with the skeleton of a horse; a female skeleton is depicted along with the sketeton of an ostrich. The analogies intended are plain to see. The female skeleton, in particular, has a greatly elongated neck and much exaggerated pelvis.

Anatomical theory was (and still is) in the business of accounting for the phenomena. What diagrams like these of the male and female skeletons do is badly skew the relevant evidence that those theories should be explaining.

Examples like these from Wilson and from Scheibinger show how easy it is to get values into science. (There are, of course, many different ways of getting values into science; via phenomena is just one more route.) The task for theorizers is doubly complicated: not only do they have to worry about their theories doing justice to the phenomena, but they must also be concerned that the alleged phenomena are doing justice to reality.

THOUGHT EXPERIMENTS

Thought experiments deal with phenomena. Obviously, they don't deal with actual experimental data – this much is true by definition. But the fact that they involve picturable processes suggests that we need to keep something observation-like centrally involved when we try to understand them.

In Einstein's elevator, to cite one important example, the observer inside cannot tell whether she is in a gravitational field or accelerating. A beam of light passing through would bend downward if the elevator were accelerating, so, by the principle of equivalence, it would also bend downward in a gravitational field (Figure 12). The conditions required to make such an observation are so extreme that any actual observer would be a

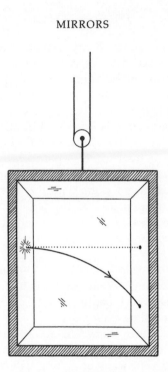

Figure 12

puddle on the floor of the elevator. The observation in this thought experiment is of phenomena, not data.

Newton's bucket thought experiment (Figure 13) provides an instructive example in a different way. The thought experiment asks us to imagine the different stages of a bucket partly filled with water as it is released and allowed to 'rotate'. The water and bucket would be initially at rest with respect to one another, and the water surface is flat. Next they would be in relative motion. In the third stage they would again be at rest with respect to one another, but this time the surface of the water would be concave.

Why the difference between stages one and three? Newton's explanation is simply this: in the first stage the water and bucket are at rest with respect to absolute space, and in the third they are rotating with respect to absolute space.

After Leibniz, Newton's most forceful critics were Berkeley and Mach. Did they deny that absolute space was the best explanation for the observed difference? Not really; instead,

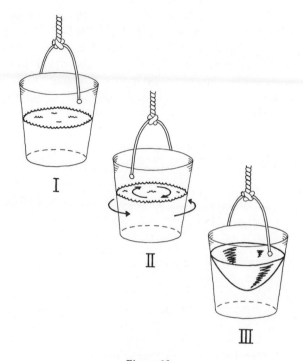

Figure 13

they denied the observed difference itself. They denied that in a universe without distant masses (the fixed stars) the water would climb the walls of the bucket. Clearly, Berkeley's and Mach's fight with Newton is not a dispute over empirical data; it is not even a fight over rival explanations of what is given in the thought experiment – it is a fight over the phenomena.

What we can see from these two thought experiments is that phenomena must be playing a role in scientific inference, a role which is distinct from that of data. Though phenomena are picturable, they exist at a high level of abstraction.

PHENOMENA AND INFERENCE

How is it possible that a great and grand theory can seem to be justified by only a tiny bit of sketchy visualized information? A lesson can be learned from a rare form of inference in mathematics. Diagrams in mathematics are usually psychological aids that help us to understand a proof. In fact, the orthodox view is that they are always psychological aids – nothing more. Real proofs, according to the common view, are derivations; they are verbal and symbolic. Pictures are never more than suggestive. But this view may be wrong. Consider the following theorem and its proof which is just a diagram. (I suggest pausing to study the diagram which will take a moment to understand.)

Theorem: $1 + 2 + 3 + \ldots + n = \dfrac{n^2}{2} + \dfrac{n}{2}$.

Proof:

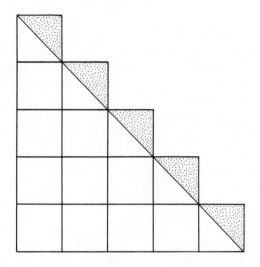

Figure 14

I wish to claim that the diagram is a perfectly good proof. One can see complete generality in the picture, even though it only illustrates the theorem for $n = 5$. The diagram does not implicitly 'suggest' a 'rigorous' verbal or symbolic proof. The regular proof of this theorem is by mathematical induction, but the diagram does not correspond to an inductive proof at all (where the key element is the passage from n to $n + 1$).

One of the morals to be drawn from this example is of great importance for the philosophy of mathematics, especially concerning the nature of proof. But the moral I want to draw here is just this: we can in special cases correctly infer theories from pictures, i.e. from visualizable situations.

The great inductive leap is really from data to phenomena; once we have the phenomena, the further inference to theory often can be actually rather small. This is because of the following feature of natural kinds.

> Any natural kind has an essential property (or set of properties) that makes it the kind that it is. If any member of a kind has essential property ϕ then every member of the kind has ϕ.

If any sample of water, for example, has chemical composition H_2O, then they all do; if any sample of gold has atomic number 79, then they all do. But notice our reluctance to make a similar inference about, say, the colour of ravens. We balk at: if any raven is black, then they all are. We hesitate because of our belief that colour is not an essential property of ravens. We do believe that all ravens are black, of course, but this belief is based on the observation of an enormous number of ravens. By contrast, our beliefs about, say, the mass of intermediate vector bosons are based on only a handful of scratchy bubble chamber photographs. So, either our physics colleagues have absurdly low standards compared with bird watchers or something remarkably different is going on in each case. Clearly, it is the latter. There is a profound difference between the two cases and it has to do with phenomena as natural kinds. In particular, if any intermediate vector boson has mass m then they all have mass m. Natural kind inference is quite different from enumerative induction, the principle used in inferring the colour of all ravens.[3]

While I have invoked natural kinds and their essential properties to account for some of the aspects of phenomena, my commitment to natural kinds is not too deep. Perhaps *pattern* would be a better notion.[4] Instead of seeing phenomena as constructed out of data, I should take patterns to be so constructed. First, patterns would avoid the controversial metaphysics of essences etc.; second, patterns are obviously abstract and hence clearly different from observable data; and third, inferences from patterns are quite unproblematic and so lend themselves to quick conclusions of the sort we see in the mathematics and thought experiment examples given above. For now, at any rate, I prefer to remain agnostic and leave this an open question, and for consistency I shall stick with talk of natural kinds.

Of course, the question arises whether we really have a natural kind (or an essential property of a natural kind) on our hands or not. Is mass really an essential property and colour not? It seems like an a priori assumption, and to some extent I dare say that it is. But the view that the colour of ravens is not an essential property while the micro-structure of water is, is at least in part based on very broad experience and the past success of various classes of theories that we hold. Theories based on micro-structure have been enormously successful while those based on colours have not. So the construction of phenomena out of data is based on more than the data themselves. It is theory-laden, but it needn't be laden with the theory that it will subsequently be used to test.

THE STRUCTURE OF DATA

At this point we should investigate what, if any, background assumptions are brought to the data in the process of constructing the phenomena. Bogen and Woodward cite a rather simple example in characterizing their view – the melting point of lead. They note that the melting point is taken to be 327°C, but that actual measurements seldom, if ever, get this value. Actual thermometer readings will be scattered around this point, and what science takes to be the true melting point (the phenomenon) is an average of the actual observed results (the data).

The interesting question is, why take the average? To see that this is not a trivial question, consider another experiment where the average is the last thing one would want to take: the Franck–Hertz experiment, which is taken to show that in collisions between electrons and atoms the transfer of energy is quantized.[5]

A glass tube contains a gas (mercury vapour); electrons are emitted by a cathode, C, at one end and accelerated by a voltage, V, toward a grid, G, which is near the other end of the tube. Many of the electrons will make it past the grid and will complete the circuit; the current will be registered on the ammeter, A. (See Figure 15.)

Franck and Hertz did not find that the current increased

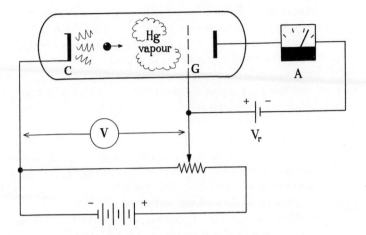

Figure 15

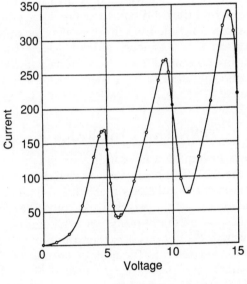

Figure 16

monotonically with the voltage. Instead they found (Figure 16) significant dips in the current at regular intervals starting at 4.9 eV.

The standard explanation for this phenomenon goes as follows. The electrons collide with the mercury atoms and give up their energy, but only in discrete amounts. The different orbits in a Bohr atom correspond to different energy levels. When a free electron collides with an atom it either loses no energy, or loses exactly the amount required to change the energy level of the atom (i.e. a bound electron moves to a higher orbit). In the case of the mercury atom it takes 4.9 eV to bump it from the ground state into the first level, and 6.7 eV to move it from the ground state to the second level. By far the most common case will be the absorption of enough energy to move or lift the atom into the first excited state; an electron will give up just enough energy for this to happen, and then continue on its way. Should it have a integral multiple of 4.9 eV then it could give up many packets of energy in its various collisions.

It is perfectly clear that if Franck and Hertz had taken the averages of their measured results it would have led to a linear relation between voltage and current. It is because they suspected quantization that they were led by their data to construct the phenomena that they did construct (as represented in the figure). So we can conclude from this case that the construction of phenomena out of data is indeed guided by some background theory. And this puts me somewhat at odds with Bogen and Woodward who take this to be a theory-laden process in *no* interesting sense.

FEYNMAN DIAGRAMS

When Richard Feynman was working on quantum electrodynamics in the late 1940s he created a set of diagrams to keep track of the monster calculations that were required. Though they were intended for his personal use only, 'Feynman diagrams' have become an enormously powerful and popular tool in all areas of high energy physics. (For a popular account see Feynman 1985.) Feynman is thought to be one of the most 'visual' of modern physicists (see Schweber 1985), and his diagrams would seem to be a paradigm example of visualization in physics. In a sense this is certainly true. But in another important sense it is quite misleading.

The transition from an initial quantum state to a final state could happen in any of a number of different ways. Each of these different ways can be represented by a diagram, and there are mathematical expressions associated with each. To calculate

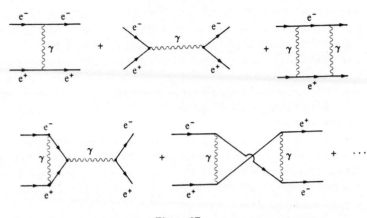

Figure 17

the final probability for the transition from one state to another, one would just calculate the expression associated with each of the diagrams. (As a practical matter, only the first few will be calculated to get a reasonably accurate answer.) Figure 17, for example, gives the first few diagrams depicting the perturbation series containing the different possible sub-processes in electron–positron scattering.

Feynman diagrams look something like cloud chamber pictures and they are often called space–time diagrams. This leads to the confusion. In fact the diagrams do not picture physical processes at all. Instead, they represent probabilities (actually, probability amplitudes). The argument for this is very simple. In quantum mechanics (as normally understood) the Heisenberg uncertainty relations imply that no particle could have a position and a momentum simultaneously, which means there are no such things as trajectories, paths, through space–time. So the lines in a Feynman diagram cannot be representations of particles and their actual paths through space–time.

So what, then, is being visualized? I think the answer is simply this: a Feynman diagram is a geometric representation of a probability function. As such it is quite different from all the other types of pictures, diagrams and illustrations I have been discussing above. It is not a picture of phenomena. Of course, visual reasoning plays a role in their use, but this is not connected to natural kind reasoning as I hold the other types to be. Instead, a Feynman diagram is more like a Venn diagram. We

139

depict, for example, that all As are Bs by representing the set of As and the set of Bs as circles, with the A-circle wholly contained within the B-circle. Clearly we can visualize the relation between the As and the Bs using the Venn diagram, but such visualization is different – though no less important – than the type of visualization involved in the construction of phenomena. In a thought experiment, for instance, we perceive the abstract natural kind; but in a Venn diagram we see some circles. Similarly, the Feynman diagram geometrically represents (often brilliantly) a mathematical function which is linked to a physical process. We see the lines in the diagram; we do not visualize the physical process itself, nor any sort of abstract version of it.

By contrast, phenomena are to be distinguished from data, the stuff of observation and experience. And even though they are relatively abstract, they have a strongly visual character. They are constructed out of data, but not just any construction will do. Phenomena are natural kinds that we can picture. As such they resemble data in a visual way that Feynman diagrams and Venn diagrams do not.

In short, the connection between illustration and inference is unusually intimate; but what I am here calling phenomena by no means exhaust visual thinking in science.

CONCLUDING REMARKS

I have not dealt with the social sciences here at all, but a cursory glance suggests the phenomena/data distinction is important here, too, perhaps even more so. Social scientists seem to do (at least) two quite distinct things. One is to establish phenomena: e.g. that there is widespread child abuse, that x per cent of the population are homosexual, that suicide rates in some cultures are higher than in others, that x per cent of women are physically abused by their male companions, that there is an x per cent unemployment rate etc. These are often extremely difficult to ascertain as we might imagine, especially when questions of sexuality are involved. The second job is to explain these phenomena. And it is indeed phenomena that social theory attempts to explain. Economists try to tell us why we have high unemployment (a downturn in the economy), not why Joe Blow is out of work (perhaps he was an incompetent worker); and

Durkheim told us why Protestant societies have higher suicide rates than Catholic ones (they are socially less cohesive); he doesn't tell us why Joe Blow killed himself (perhaps he was depressed after losing his job).

Let me now summarize the main points. Phenomena are to be distinguished from data, the stuff of observation and experience. They are relatively abstract, but have a strongly visual character. They are constructed out of data, but not just any construction will do. Phenomena are natural kinds (or patterns) that we can picture. They show up in thought experiments and they play an indispensable role in scientific inference mediating between data and theory.

The differences I have pointed out between myself and Bogen and Woodward (for example, over the theory-ladenness of phenomena) are relatively minor. The common thing is this: there are such things as phenomena; they differ from empirical data, though they do have an observable character to them; they are relatively abstract, but they bear an evidential relation to theories. What I have mainly tried to do in this chapter is tie phenomena to the abstract realm and show how some inferences (via diagrams and thought experiments) are made in that remarkable realm, so close to Plato's heart.

8

WHAT IS
THE VECTOR POTENTIAL?

Galileo had three children, Marie Curie had two. Between them they had an average of two and a half. We all know what children are, and we all know that each and every one of them is a whole child – nothing in reality corresponds to 'two and a half children'. Average families aren't theoretical entities, like electrons. We believe in electrons because we can make all sorts of wonderful predictions using them. We can do that with the average family, too – by knowing the size of the average family we can successfully predict how many day-care spaces will be needed next year, how many toys will be purchased at Christmas and how many visits will be made in July by the tooth fairy. Yet, in spite of the tremendous predictive power of 'the average family', no one is in the least tempted to say it corresponds to reality. Anti-realists think 'electron' fails to correspond to reality, too; but here at least we have a fight between plausible realist and anti-realist views – no one champions the average family. What's the difference?

The answer seems rather straightforward. We count children by mapping a set of them onto a subset of the natural numbers. Thus, the set of Marie Curie's children, {Eve, Irène}, gets mapped onto the set $\{0, 1\} = 2$. Any (not too big) set of natural numbers corresponds to some possible family. But the natural numbers are a part of the real numbers, and this fact is exploited in the creation of such physically unrealistic entities as the average family when we form $(2 + 3)/2 = 2\frac{1}{2}$. For this reason, not even the most realist-minded among us is tempted to see the average family as anything but a mathematical artifact.

When Faraday and Maxwell were creating what we now call classical electrodynamics, they faced a similar situation. Both were quite happy to believe in the reality of charged bodies – even unseen ones. But what is the status of the field? Is it a real thing, like a charged body, or just an extremely useful mathematical device, like the average family?

The considerations which tipped the balance in favour of a realistic view of fields were two: conservation of energy and the finite propagation in time of electromagnetic interactions. Maxwell, when complaining about action at a distance theories, remarked:

> Now we are unable to conceive of propagation in time, except as the flight of a material substance through space, or as the propagation of a condition of motion or stress in a medium already existing in space. . . . But in all of these [action at a distance] theories the question naturally occurs:– If something is transmitted from one particle to another at a distance, what is its condition after it has left the one particle and before it has reached the other?
>
> (1891, §866)

In another place Maxwell was quite emphatic:

> In speaking of the energy of the field, however, I wish to be understood literally. All energy is the same as mechanical energy, whether it exists in the form of motion, or in that of elasticity, or in any other form. The energy in electro-magnetic phenomena is mechanical energy. The only question is, Where does it reside? On the old theories it resides in the electrified bodies, conducting circuits, and magnets, in the form of an unknown quality called potential energy, or the power of producing certain effects at a distance. On our theory it resides in the electro-magnetic field, in the space surrounding the electrified and magnetic bodies, as well as in those bodies themselves, and is in two different forms, which may be described without hypothesis as magnetic polarization, or, according to a very probable hypothesis, as the motion and the strain of one and the same medium.
>
> (1890, vol. I, 563)

We can put these remarks together to produce an explicit argument of considerable power for the reality of the electromagnetic field.[1] Consider a system of two isolated electrified bodies; one body is jiggled and after a delay the other wiggles in response.

1 Energy is conserved and localized (i.e. its magnitude remains constant and it is located in some entity or other).
2 Electro-magnetic interaction is propagated with a finite velocity.
3 The total energy of the system will be located in the electrified bodies at the start and at the end of an interaction; but not at intermediate times.
4 Therefore the energy at intermediate times must be located elsewhere, i.e. in the electro-magnetic field.
5 Therefore the electro-magnetic field is physically real (and not just a useful mathematical device).

This is a beautiful line of reasoning, as convincing as these things can get. Faraday and Maxwell were persuaded by this type of consideration, and both were realists about the electro-magnetic field right from the start. But we can better appreciate the power of the argument by seeing that it does *not* work in the case of the Newtonian gravitational field. (Discriminating arguments are sometimes more plausible than those like 'inference to the best explanation' which tend to make everything real.) The reason for the *ineffectiveness* of the argument in the gravitational case is simple: gravitational interactions are instantaneous; so the total energy will always be located in some body or other. Consequently, in the case of Newtonian (but not relativistic) gravitation, it would still be reasonable to hold the view that the field is nothing more than a mathematical fiction.

Agnosticism, I have so far suggested, is the right attitude toward Newton's gravitation field. Others, such as Einstein, have taken an even dimmer view. In their justly famous popular work, *The Evolution of Physics* (1938), Einstein and Infeld include a drawing to represent the Newtonian gravitational field (Figure 18). They remark:

Some may, perhaps, find it helpful to regard these lines as something more than a drawing, and to imagine the real actions of force passing through them. This may be done, but then the speed of the actions along the lines of force must be assumed as infinitely great! The forces between two bodies, according to Newton's laws, depends only on

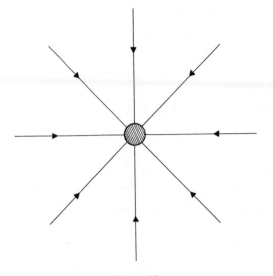

Figure 18

distance; time does not enter the picture. The force has to pass from one body to another in no time! But, as motion with infinite speed cannot mean much to any reasonable person, any attempt to make our drawing something more than a model leads nowhere.

(1938, 127f.)

It has been well over a century since the realist considerations for fields were first proposed, but our contemporaries seem to hold similar views. Richard Feynman, for example, writes: 'The fact that the electro-magnetic field can possess momentum and energy makes that field very real . . .' (1963, vol. I, ch. 10, 9). (By contrast, Newtonian gravitational fields could never hold energy or momentum.) Not all, however, get the argument quite right. In their otherwise splendid book, *The Classical Theory of Fields* (1975, 43), Landau and Lifshitz say that the finite velocity of interaction implies the 'physical reality' of the field. Not so. A finite velocity is neither necessary nor sufficient. It is not necessary, since a rigid Newtonian rod pushed on one end transmits a continuous action instantly to the other. It is not sufficient either, since clearly it is *logically* possible for one event to cause another at some later time. The argument for the reality of fields only works by assuming both premisses: finite velocity of interaction *and* conservation of energy.

Of course, instrumentalists and other anti-realists are likely to be quite unimpressed with all of this – and understandably so. This argument for the reality of the electro-magnetic field is really only for the benefit of those who are happy with theoretical entities, in principle, and who simply want to know which terms correspond to something real ('children' and 'electro-magnetic fields') and which terms don't ('average families' and 'gravitational fields').

Maxwell's theory of electro-magnetic fields is embodied in his famous equations. Let's briefly review these.

$$\text{I} \qquad \nabla \cdot E \qquad = \quad \frac{\rho}{\epsilon_0}$$

$$\text{II} \qquad \nabla \times E \qquad = \quad \frac{-\partial B}{\partial t}$$

$$\text{III} \qquad \nabla \cdot B \qquad = \quad 0$$

$$\text{IV} \qquad c^2 \nabla \times B \qquad = \quad \frac{j}{\epsilon_0} + \frac{\partial E}{\partial t}$$

The first of these is known as Gauss's law. It relates the divergence of the electric field through a surface to the charge contained inside. (ρ is the charge density and ϵ has to do with the medium; in our case we are only concerned with free space, hence ϵ_0.) The second is Faraday's law of magnetic induction which relates the strength of an electric field to a changing magnetic field. The third equation says, in effect, that there are no magnetic monopoles; unlike electrons and protons, which have either a negative or a positive charge, magnetic bodies always have a north and a south pole, so their field lines are always closed loops. The final equation is a generalization of Ampere's law; like Faraday's law, it relates the electric to the magnetic field; in particular, it says that the properties of the magnetic field are due to electric currents or to changing electric fields, or both. (j is the current and c is a constant of proportionality which famously turns out to be the same as the velocity of light.)

By the argument above, the E field and the B field are real. That is, E and B denote real physical things; they are not mere mathematical fictions. But what about some of the other fancy items of electrodynamics? In particular, what about the *vector potential*? Is it just a mathematical entity like the average family, or is there a real field corresponding to it as well?

The vector potential arises initially as a purely mathematical result: When the divergence of a vector field B is zero, then there is another vector field A such that $B = \nabla \times A$. The third of Maxwell's equations then implies the existence of the A field, known as the vector potential. This is all secured by an elementary fact about vectors, namely $\nabla \cdot (\nabla \times A) = 0$.

The way in which the A field is conjured into existence suggests that it is merely a mathematical artifact, just as lacking in flesh and blood as the average family. Since the beginning of electrodynamics, this was the common attitude.[2] Hendrik Lorentz called the vector potential an 'auxiliary function' (1915/1952, 19) which he introduces to make calculations easier. Feynman says that 'for a long time it was believed that A was not a "real" field' (1963, vol. II, §15, 8). And most recently Leslie Ballentine remarks, 'the vector and scalar potentials were introduced as convenient mathematical aids for calculating the electric and magnetic fields. Only the fields and not the potentials, were regarded as having physical significance' (1990, 220).

So why would anyone think otherwise? That is, why think of A as physically real? The change in attitude toward the vector potential comes from considering its role in a simple quantum mechanical case. A remarkable result known as the Aharonov–Bohm effect has made the difference; now the received wisdom has it that the A field is just as real as any other. Let's turn to the details of the Aharonov–Bohm effect to see why there has been such a change of heart.

From a purely *classical* point of view, the vector potential plays no physically significant role at all. The Lorentz force law is $F = q(E + v \times B)$, which means that the force on a charged particle depends only on the E and B fields (as well as on charge q and velocity v). So even if the A field should have a non-zero value at some point occupied by the charged particle, it would have no physical effect. In a solenoid, for example, the value of the B field outside the solenoid is zero, but the A field has a non-zero value (Figure 19). In cylindrical coordinates (r, ϕ, z), the components of the B field are as follows.

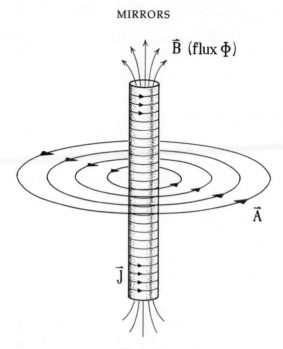

Figure 19

Inside the solenoid: $B_r = B_\phi = 0$, $B_z = B$ where $B = |\mathbf{B}|$
Outside the solenoid: $B_r = B_\phi = B_z = 0$

The components of the vector potential, however, are as follows.

Inside $A_r = A_z = 0$, $A_\phi = Br/2$
Outside $A_r = A_z = 0$, $A_\phi = BR^2/2r$ where R is the radius of the solenoid

In spite of this, a classically charged particle in the vicinity of such a solenoid wouldn't feel a thing; it would pass by as if the solenoid wasn't there, utterly indifferent to the intensity of the *A* field.

However, in a quantum mechanical setting this is no longer true. Consider the usual split-screen device that is commonly used in quantum mechanics to illustrate interference effects. We set things up in the usual way except that behind the two-slit barrier there is a solenoid (coming out of the page). When the current is off, the interference pattern on the back screen is the usual one. But when the current is turned on the interference

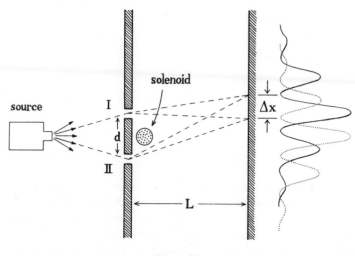

Figure 20

pattern is shifted. The **B** field is everywhere zero except inside the solenoid, but the **A** field has a non-zero value outside the solenoid; the more intense it is, the greater the shift in the interference pattern. This is the Aharonov–Bohm effect. The set-up is shown in Figure 20.

The phase difference of the electrons (with wavelength λ arriving from the two slits is $\delta = 2\pi x d/L\lambda$ (see Figure 20). Let the flux through the solenoid be Φ. The state of a free electron is $\psi = \exp\{i/\hbar(\mathbf{p}\cdot\mathbf{r})\}$. As a result of moving through the **A** field there is a change of phase

$$\psi \rightarrow \psi' = \exp\left(\frac{i}{\hbar}\, \mathbf{p}\cdot\mathbf{r} - \frac{ie}{\hbar}\, \mathbf{A}\cdot\mathbf{r}\right).$$

Over the entire trajectory the phase change is

$$\Delta\theta = \frac{-e}{\hbar} \int_{\mathrm{I+II}} \mathbf{A} \cdot d\mathbf{r}$$

The change in the phase difference δ can now be calculated.

$$\Delta\delta = \Delta\theta_{\mathrm{I}} - \Delta\theta_{\mathrm{II}}$$

$$= -\frac{e}{\hbar} \int_{\mathrm{I}} \mathbf{A} \cdot d\mathbf{r} - \frac{-e}{\hbar} \int_{\mathrm{II}} \mathbf{A} \cdot d\mathbf{r}$$

$$= \frac{e}{\hbar} \oint_{\mathrm{II-I}} \mathbf{A} \cdot d\mathbf{r}$$

$$= \frac{e}{\hbar} \int_{\mathrm{II-I}} \nabla \times \mathbf{A} \cdot \mathrm{d}\mathbf{S}$$

$$= \frac{e}{\hbar} \int \mathbf{B} \cdot \mathrm{d}\mathbf{S}$$

$$= \frac{e}{\hbar} \Phi.$$

The interference pattern then shifts by the amount

$$\Delta x = \frac{L\lambda \, \Delta\delta}{2\pi\mathrm{d}} = \frac{L\lambda e\Phi}{2\pi\mathrm{d}\hbar}.$$

There is no question about the argument from a theoretical point of view: the combined formalisms of classical field theory and of quantum mechanics certainly lead to this predicted outcome. Moreover, there have been some recent experiments of remarkable sensitivity that have detected the effect.[3] So the problem now is entirely one of interpretation: how are we to understand the $\mathbf{A}$ field? Is it a mathematical artifact? A real field? Or something else?

The overwhelming opinion seems now to be this: the $\mathbf{A}$ field is not just a computational device (like the average family); rather, it is a *physically real field*, just as real as the $\mathbf{E}$ and $\mathbf{B}$ fields. In the words of those who initiated this very plausible argument:

> In quantum theory, an electron (for example) can be influenced by the potentials even if all the field regions are excluded from it. In other words, in a field-free multiply-connected region of space, the physical properties of the system still depend on the potentials. . . . the potentials must, in certain cases, be considered as physically effective, even when there are no fields acting on the charged particles.
>
> (Aharonov and Bohm 1959, 490)

(Note that for Aharonov and Bohm 'field' means only $\mathbf{B}$ or $\mathbf{E}$ while $\mathbf{A}$ is a 'potential'. I am following the common practice of calling $\mathbf{A}$ a field, too.)

Interpreting the vector potential as a physically real field is one way to deal with the Aharonov–Bohm effect. Another way is often mentioned, only to be dismissed. The alternative is to take the magnetic field as causally responsible for the effect, but to allow that it is acting at a distance. Of course, it seems almost self-contradictory to say that a field is acting at a distance, but there is no logical problem with this. The B field is confined within the solenoid, but it might (like a massive particle in Newtonian gravitation theory) act where it is not. Thus, in this view, it is the real B field, not the unreal A field, that causes the phase shift in the interference pattern – but it does so *at a distance*.

Such an interpretation is dismissed out of hand as a gross violation of the proper spirit of modern physics:

> according to current relativistic notions, all fields must interact only locally. And since the electrons cannot reach the regions where the fields are, we cannot interpret such effects as due to the fields [i.e. E or B] themselves.
>
> (Aharonov and Bohm 1959, 490)

> In our sense then, the A field is 'real.' You might say: 'But there *was* a magnetic field.' There was, but remember our original idea – that a field is 'real' if it is what must be specified *at the position* of the particle in order to get the motion. The B field [in the solenoid] acts at a distance. If we want to describe its influence not as action-at-a-distance, we must use the vector potential.
>
> (Feynman 1963, vol. II, §15, 12)

So our options in accounting for the Aharonov–Bohm effect appear to be the following.

1 A non-local effect of the magnetic field B. This has the advantage of evoking something to which we already ascribe physical reality; but it has the disadvantage of involving action at a distance. This interpretation is universally rejected, and rightly so.

2 A local effect of the vector potential, A. This account of the Aharonov–Bohm effect is universally favoured since it is in the spirit of field theory. Once we're over our initial shock – and it is a shock – we're happy to give up the idea that the vector potential is merely an auxiliary function and we cheerfully ascribe physical reality to it.

Superficially, the considerations surrounding the A field are like those concerning the reality of the E and B fields. However, the similarity is only superficial. There are significant difficulties with taking the vector potential to be a physically real field. Let's turn to these and see why the much favoured second interpretation is at least as problematic as the first.

The first problem with taking the A field seriously has to do with gauge invariance. This problem is already well known, so I shall only quickly review it here. Suppose two potentials are related by a gauge transformation: $A \rightarrow A' = A + \nabla f$ (where f is any appropriate scalar function). Relevant mathematical operations performed on either A or A' lead to identical consequences. For instance, the curl of A is the same as the curl of A', and the line integral of either around a closed path has the same value. In short, they cannot be distinguished physically; both give rise to exactly the same phase shift. It seems hard to believe that one of the infinitely many different vector potentials is the right one, the one that is the genuine real field responsible for the Aharonov–Bohm effect.

The second problem with taking A seriously has to do with locality. It seems that the great virtue of the vector potential is that it (unlike the magnetic field) acts *locally* on the electrons in the interference set-up, whereas the B field would have to act non-locally. This is indeed true in the normal version of the experiment. However, it is possible to introduce non-local effects into the situation by simply modifying the experiment into one involving a kind of delayed-choice.[4] In what follows I shall only sketch a result due to van Kampen. (See his 1984 paper for details.)

First, a distinction. There are two senses of locality; the A field is local in one sense but not the other. The sense in which it is local is the sense in which it acts only where it is. In this sense, the B field, which is totally inside the solenoid, would be acting in a non-local way if it acted on the electrons outside the solenoid. The second sense of locality has to do with velocity; something is non-local if it interacts (even through a continuous medium) at a speed greater than the velocity of light. The A field is non-local in this second sense. (The two senses of non-locality are related by the theory of relativity. By placing an upper bound on the velocity of interactions, special relativity – with the help of the conservation of energy – imposes field theory upon us; i.e. it implies the existence of a field, the medium of transmission of any interaction.)

Let us now see how the A field can be non-local in the second sense (thereby violating special relativity).

In the normal double slit version of the Aharonov–Bohm effect, we either have the current in the solenoid *off* (and it stays off when we fire the electrons, resulting in some specific interference pattern) or we have the current *on* (and it stays on when the electrons are fired, resulting in the interference pattern being shifted). In a delayed-choice version of this experiment we start with the current off and wait until the electrons are almost to the back screen. Then we turn the current on. The value of the *A* field changes *immediately* and the effect on the interference pattern on the back screen is *instantaneous*.

It would seem we could send signals using such a device – thereby experimentally upsetting the relativity of simultaneity. However, there is an exactly compensating phase shift, the *electric* Aharonov–Bohm effect. When the flux in the solenoid changes, the electric field *E* connected with the *increasing* flux Φ creates a potential difference between the source and the screen,

$$\int_{source}^{screen} E \cdot ds,$$

even though *E* itself does not act near the screen. The phase difference that this gives rise to is $\Delta\delta = -e/\hbar\Phi$, which is exactly the opposite of that due to the magnetic effect. (I stress that all of this happens only in the delayed-choice version of the experiment; when the flux is turned on before the electron reaches the solenoid, the usual phase shift is detected.)

It might be thought that since this leads to no possible observable effect, non-locality here is a non-issue. However, I take it that there is a world of difference – though completely unobservable – between a particle with no forces acting on it and one with a pair of equal but opposite forces acting on it. Instrumentalists may be inclined to dismiss the difference, but anyone prepared to accept the physical reality of the vector potential must also accept the existence of an instantaneous effect.

This is certainly a case of action at a distance in that it is a flagrant violation of special relativity – *if the A field is taken to be physically real*. On the other hand, an instantaneous change in the intensity of *A* everywhere would be harmless, if *A* were taken to be no more than a mathematical artifact. (The instant a new baby is born *anywhere*, the size of the average family changes *everywhere*.)

The instantaneous character of the vector potential is not

shared by the other fields we consider real. For example, a magnetic field created by a current which is suddenly turned on changes its intensity only with finite velocity c. The A field does not carry energy or momentum, which makes it quite unlike the electric or magnetic fields; instead its non-local character makes it much more like the Newtonian gravitational field, something which is much more plausibly understood to be a mere mathematical artifact.

In sum, it is quite implausible to take the A field as a *physically real field*. This interpretation of the Aharonov–Bohm effect, though it is certainly the most popular, is actually no better than the one which has B acting non-locally. And it is possibly even worse since they both have action at a distance problems, but at least the B field enjoys an independent argument for its existence. Neither is a happy solution. We need a different approach.

I shall now sketch out an alternative which will employ the realist conception of *laws of nature* that I outlined above in Chapter 6. So let me begin with a brief review of what a natural law is.

The salient features of the realist view of laws of nature are as follows.

1 Laws are relations between abstract entities.
2 They are real, but exist outside of space and time.
3 Laws are causally responsible for the regularities that do obtain in the physical world.

Let me turn from considering laws for a moment to focus on the mathematical representation of classical mechanics and quantum mechanics.

A single particle in classical mechanics is represented mathematically by a phase space. This has a total of six dimensions which are associated with the three spatial coordinates and the corresponding three momenta, $q_1, q_2, q_3, p_1, p_2, p_3$. A function H, known as the Hamiltonian, is defined on these. In the simple case of a conservative system, the Hamiltonian is just the total energy, $H = T + V$. The behaviour of the system (its trajectory through phase space) is fully specified by Hamilton's equations:

$$\frac{\mathrm{d}p_i}{\mathrm{d}t} = \frac{-\partial H}{\partial q_i}$$

$$\frac{\mathrm{d}q_i}{\mathrm{d}t} = \frac{\partial H}{\partial p_i}$$

The *state* of a classical mechanical system is represented by a point $x = (q_1, q_2, q_3, p_1, p_2, p_3)$ in phase space. Notice the choice of words. What does 'represent' mean? Are we to take 'state' seriously, as a thing in its own right? That is, should we take the state as identical to a mathematical entity, or rather as a thing in its own right which is *represented* by a mathematical entity but not reducible to it? It seems pretty clear that the classical state has no life of its own. There is a physical system with a position and a momentum, and there is a complete representation of this system in phase space. There is no need for a third kind of thing – the state of the system – over and above the physical properties of the system. The classical state can be completely identified with the point in phase space; it is nothing but a mathematical entity. Can the same be said for the quantum mechanical state?

The quantum state is usually introduced through the following postulate: The state of a quantum system is represented by a vector ψ in a Hilbert space. The important question is this: is the 'quantum state' just a *façon de parler* in the same way that the 'classical state' is? The answer is no.

The classical state corresponds to a point in phase space – but the coordinates of this point correspond exactly to the physical properties of the physical system. There is no such correspondence in the quantum case. The quantum state is not reducible either to the physical system or to the mathematical model (as it is in classical mechanics). It is very easy to be misled by the standard terminology of quantum mechanics, since 'ψ' is used for both *the state* and *the vector which represents that state*. The quantum state is neither physical nor mathematical – it is a unique sort of abstract entity.

From a mathematical point of view I see the difference as follows. In classical mechanics the mathematical model is a direct representation of the physical system. But in quantum mechanics mathematics hooks on at a higher level of abstraction (Figure 21). Instead of representing a physical system, the Hilbert space represents the *state* of the physical system. Explanations of physical events can be very misleading. Often a lot of esoteric mathematics is involved making it seem that

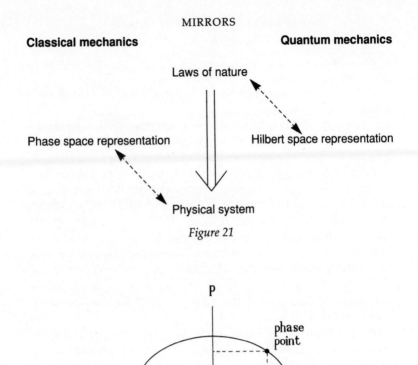

Classical mechanics   **Quantum mechanics**

Laws of nature

Phase space representation   Hilbert space representation

Physical system

Figure 21

Figure 22

mathematics is doing the explaining. Not so. Mathematics explains nothing – it is causally inert. Mathematics represents or models the situation. The real causes are the laws of nature. In classical mechanics laws are *indirectly* represented by mathematical structures, but in quantum mechanics the mathematics hooks *directly* onto the abstract laws themselves, and only indirectly onto the physical world. Normally we take Hamilton's equations or the Schrödinger equation to be laws of nature. Strictly, they are not – they are *representations* of laws of nature (indirect and direct representations, respectively).

I shall illustrate this with schematic examples. Suppose we

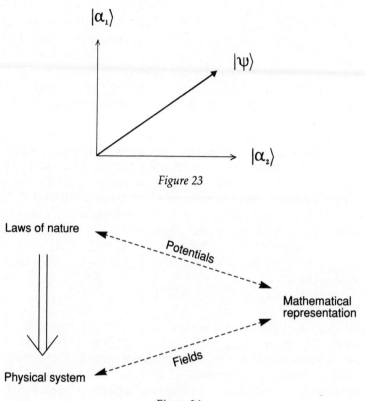

Figure 23

Figure 24

have a classical one-dimensional harmonic oscillator. Its state is some point on an orbit (corresponding to some energy E) in phase space (Figure 22). The system is governed by Hamilton's equations, which can be said to express the law; there is no need to posit a state as a *real* thing over and above the physical properties of position and momentum. The relevant law of nature is about the oscillator's position and momentum – in no serious sense is it about its state.

By contrast, the possible properties of a quantum system, α_1, $\alpha_2, \ldots$, are associated with the eigenvectors $|\alpha_1\rangle$, $|\alpha_2\rangle, \ldots$ of an operator defined on the representing Hilbert space. The state of the system is represented by a vector ψ which is in general a superposition of eigenvectors (Figure 23). For a multitude of well-known reasons, we cannot simply associate the state with the actually existing properties of the quantum system. My claim is as follows. (1) The classical state is a purely mathematical object, a function of the mathematical representation of the actual properties of the physical system. (2) The quantum state is a non-physical property of the physical system. It is a component of a law of nature, an abstract entity. The relevant law of nature (which is represented by – but not identical to – the Schrödinger equation, $H\psi = (-i/\hbar)\,\partial\psi/\partial t$) governs the physical system.

Having made these points (all too briefly and somewhat dogmatically, I confess), let us now turn back to the vector potential. My suggestion is this. The vector potential is neither a mathematical artifact (like the average family) nor a physically real field (like the electro-magnetic field). Instead, it is an abstract entity (like a quantum state), a component of a law of nature, and represented mathematically by the vector field A.

The point may be further clarified by analogy with the history of interpretations of ψ. When Schrödinger first proposed his wave mechanics, he understood ψ to be a physically real wave. This is similar to the reigning view of the A field in the light of the Aharonov–Bohm effect. Max Born, however, took ψ to be a probability wave, a mere mathematical entity. This is like the pre-Aharonov–Bohm view of the vector potential. Of course, neither view of ψ turned out to be correct. Many people today would perhaps be happy to follow Heisenberg who said that ψ 'represents a mixture of two things, partly a fact and partly our knowledge of a fact' (1958, 45). While I wish to remain as far as possible from this or any other variation on the Copenhagen theme, there is one similarity between the Copenhagen interpretation and how I see the vector potential: both reject understanding ψ/A as either straightforwardly mathematical or straightforwardly physical. There is a third kind of thing in the universe: it is not mathematical, but it is abstract; it is not physical, but it plays a causally determining role in how the physical world works.

My suggestion solves two problems and creates a new one. The advantages are these. The vector potential is causally efficacious in that it is responsible for (and so explains) the Aharonov–Bohm effect. An abstract entity such as this can have causal powers that no mathematical entity will have. Second, there is no problem with violations of locality. Being *outside* of space–time the vector potential does not transmit signals at any velocity.

The disadvantage is obvious. I have explained the obscure and paradoxical ontology of the vector potential by appeal to an even more obscure and paradoxical ontology of quantum states, abstract entities and laws of nature – hardly a clarification of the issue. Conceded – but I am unrepentant. My hope is that noting the similarity between the quantum state and the vector potential will, at the very least, help to shed a tiny bit of light on each.

9

PROOF AND TRUTH IN THE ABSTRACT REALM

Proofs and Refutations (1976) (*PR*) is Imre Lakatos's only book[1] and what a wonderful book it is. This masterpiece generates great excitement as it traces the history of the Descartes–Euler conjecture that, for any polyhedron, the number of vertices minus the number of edges plus the number of faces equals two ($V - E + F = 2$). Lakatos keeps the reader as near the edge of the seat as is possible in a work on the philosophy of mathematics. We wonder: how will it turn out in the end? But the moral is: there is no end. The conjecture is not now settled and never will be, if 'settled' means established for all time. The reason that it is unsettled is certainly not for lack of trying. And more important, it is not for the lack of a proof or for lack of a counter-example either. The conjecture has been proved *and* refuted many times. Rather, claims Lakatos, mathematical knowledge does not accumulate as we have traditionally thought; 'mathematics does not grow through a monotonous increase of the number of indubitably established theorems but through the incessant improvement of guesses by speculation and criticism' (*PR*, 5); it grows by what Lakatos calls 'the method of proofs and refutations'. It is an account of mathematics which makes it look much more like science in two respects. Mathematics is fallible, not certain. And mathematics is objective; it describes something real. But Lakatos's mathematics is still a priori – in spite of his insistence on calling it 'empirical'.

It is this combination of reasons – objective, fallible, a priori – which makes his account of mathematics so interesting. It also makes it a model for how I want to view (part of) the natural sciences. The whole story, it is not; but there is much wisdom in

160

Lakatos's work on mathematics that can be transferred to the non-mathematical (but still abstract) realm.

Lakatos sees formalism as the dominant philosophy and, in fact, as the despised logical positivism of mathematics. But formalism is not the only enemy – his attack is much broader. Anyone who holds the view that we are accumulating ever more *infallible* mathematics also comes under fire. This includes traditional platonists, Brouwerian Intuitionists and sundry others. All infallibilists are lumped together under the heading 'Euclidean'. It is this Euclideanism which comes under the most severe attack in *PR*, an assault which it may not be able to withstand.

PR is a work of great literary merit; it is in the form of a dialogue among teacher and students. It is also a 'rational reconstruction' of two hundred years in the history of mathematics, specifically, the history of the conjecture that $V - E + F = 2$ for any polyhedra, a problem central to the development of combinatorial topology. The 'actual' history, says Lakatos, is contained in the footnotes which are extensive and an integral part of the whole. It is all fascinating.

The work in one sense is difficult to understand – just when readers think they have Lakatos's position down, something to contradict it is found. The problem is partly the dialogue format. Unlike a platonic dialogue where Socrates is the sole mouthpiece for Plato, most participants at some time or other speak for Lakatos. Doubtless, the employment of this literary mode stems from his (Popperian) view that we make advances through the criticism of conjectures. Accordingly, inquiry is much more of a group activity; everyone contributes and all change their views from time to time. Though admirable, such open-mindedness on the part of the dialogue's participants can be aggravating for the reader – but this is a minor problem, not to be exaggerated.

Lakatos is one of those who sees an intimate connection between history and philosophy. He paraphrases Kant: 'the history of mathematics, lacking the guidance of philosophy, has become *blind*, while the philosophy of mathematics, turning its back on the most intriguing phenomena in the history of mathematics, has become empty' (*PR*, 2). Above all, it is the history of mathematics – rationally reconstructed – that Lakatos uses to hammer away at anyone who is not a fallibilist. We have ignored history at our peril; and those who have paid attention to the history of mathematics have been for the most part, Lakatos suggests, philosophically inept; he calls them 'unhistorical historians'. *PR* contains lessons for philosophers and historians alike.

It has pedagogical consequences too. Lakatos thinks mathematics would be much easier to learn if textbooks were written historically. Definitions, theorems and counter-examples would all be more readily grasped if only they were presented to the learner within the problem situation in which they first arose. Textbooks and historical tomes would then come to have a character surprisingly similar to one another. Though limited, this is already done to some extent. Texts on set theory, for example, motivate (the current version of) the axiom of comprehension with a discussion of Russell's paradox. Lakatos simply wants this greatly extended so that each and every move is motivated by the problems which preceded it. This will certainly make presentations longer than they are normally; but Lakatos thinks this will be more than compensated for by the fact that, since everything will be so natural, it will be more quickly mastered and built upon.

Yet there are other reasons for presenting mathematics historically. According to Lakatos, this is really the only way a mathematical theory can be evaluated. No isolated theory can be judged true or false. The unit of appraisal is not the single theory; it is the *change* of theory. The proper way to evaluate any theory is to see if it is an improvement, a progressive shift over its predecessor. 'The power of the theory', he remarks, 'lies in its capacity to explain its refutations in the course of its growth' (*PR*, 94). Appreciating its virtues means appreciating its past; accordingly, the history of mathematics is essential to the evaluation of present day mathematics.[2]

Of course, history, to be useful, should be accurate. But after reading *PR* readers will be left with the feeling that many standard histories are woefully inadequate. They are commonly written with the view that a theorem, once proved, is settled for eternity. They present mathematics as a history of the accumulation of *certain* knowledge. Events of the past which do not fit this mould are passed off as aberrations which have at most, anecdotal significance. Even readers who do not find themselves generally sympathetic to Lakatos will have to admit that the present state of the historiography of mathematics is quite

162

unsatisfactory. Whig history of science is almost everywhere in disgrace, but the Whig spirit unfortunately still flourishes in mathematics. *PR* makes it manifestly clear that some changes in our view of the mathematical past are desperately needed.

PR is a masterpiece. It is also, as I mentioned above, a model for how I see science. In the balance of this chapter I want to investigate some of its central themes, in particular the nature of proofs and of definitions and ontology. My aims are two: the first is simply to discuss a wonderful book. The second aim is to connect it with my own views on the natural sciences. As I argued above, abstract entities and the a priori play a big role. In all of this it is important to have the right view of mathematical reality itself. Lakatos's combination of platonism and fallibilism is just about right.

PROOFS

Mathematical proof – what is it? How does it work? What does it do? These are perhaps the central questions of *PR*. To see Lakatos's view of proof more clearly, I shall contrast it with two others. Formalists take a proof to be a sequence of statements, starting from postulates and ending in a statement of the theorem, where each step obeys the rules of logic. What a proof does is simply establish that

$\vdash$ Axioms $\supset$ Theorem

is a logical truth. Of course, actual proofs don't look like this at all; they are taken to be informal sketches of real proofs, sketches that could in principle be fleshed out. Moreover, it is a consequence of this view that one could never show any axiom to be true, since there is no way to prove the axioms, except, of course, the trivial way of deriving them from themselves.

G. H. Hardy provides a second, rather picturesque alternative. His view of proof is pure platonism.

> I have myself always thought of a mathematician as in the first instance an *observer*, a man who gazes at a distant range of mountains and notes down his observations. His object is simply to distinguish clearly and notify to others as many different peaks as he can. . . . there is, strictly, no such thing as mathematical proof; that we can, in the last analysis, do nothing but *point*; that proofs are what

Littlewood and I call *gas*, rhetorical flourishes designed to affect psychology . . .

(Hardy 1929, 18)

When it comes to the presentation of mathematics, the platonist will probably write up proofs in the same fashion as the formalist. The real difference is in their attitudes to the axioms and the consequences of those axioms – platonists believe them; formalists don't.

Both of these are examples of Euclideanism, according to Lakatos. They each start out with infallible axioms, then step after infallible step arrive at an infallible theorem. (The axioms are infallibly true, according to some platonists; they are inviolable conventions, according to some formalists.) Such Euclideanism, says Lakatos, is totally misguided; the history of mathematics makes a mockery of it.

But for a platonist like Hardy there is more to it than merely believing that the axioms are true. There are three claims implicit in the passage just quoted:

1 mathematical statements refer to a realm of mathematical objects which *exist* independently of us;
2 our mathematical knowledge is based (in part) on a kind of *perception*;
3 when we have a clear view we can be *certain* that what we see is true.

It is really only the third of these that Lakatos has a case against; his view is quite compatible with a fallible version of platonism.

To Lakatos a proof is much more than a device used to justify mathematical assertions. Proofs are the central contrivance in what he calls *the method of proofs and refutations*. It is at once a method both *descriptive* and *prescriptive*; it is an account of the best mathematics of the past, and so, it is also a guide for research in the future. The method is Lakatos's general heuristic guide to mathematical discovery.

First, a primitive conjecture is made, such as, that $V - E + F = 2$ holds for any polyhedron. Then a proof is given. Standards of proof are constantly changing, so that what a proof is could, in principle, be almost anything. It is usually some sort of argument, or as Lakatos likes to call it, a thought experiment. Often the proof takes the form of breaking things up into

164

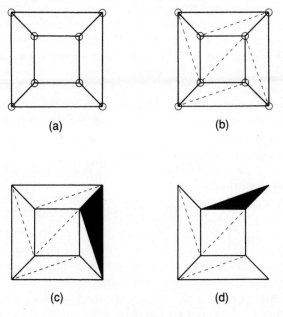

(a)   (b)

(c)   (d)

Figure 25

lemmas or subconjectures (which are tentatively accepted) and of showing that these lemmas imply the initial conjecture.

Teacher: . . . I have [a proof]. It consists of the following thought-experiment. *Step 1:* Let us imagine the polyhedron to be hollow, with a surface made of thin rubber. If we cut out one of the faces we can stretch the remaining surface flat on the blackboard, without tearing it. The faces and edges will be deformed, the edges may become curved, but V and E will not alter, so that if and only if $V - E + F = 2$ for the original polyhedron, $V - E + F = 1$ for this flat network – remember that we have removed one face. [Figure 25(a) shows the flat network for the case of the cube.] *Step 2:* We now triangulate our map – it does indeed look like a geographical map. We draw (possibly curvilinear) diagonals in those (possibly curvilinear) polygons which are not already (possibly curvilinear) triangles. By drawing each diagonal we increase both E and F by one, so that the total $V - E + F$ will not be altered [Figure 25(b)].

165

Step 3: From the triangulated network we now remove the triangles one by one. To remove a triangle we either remove an edge – upon which one face and one edge disappear [Figure 25(c)], or we remove two edges and a vertex – upon which one face, two edges and one vertex disappear [Figure 25(d)]. Thus if $V - E + F = 1$ before a triangle is removed, it remains so after the triangle is removed. At the end of this procedure we get a single triangle. For this $V - E + F = 1$ holds true. Thus we have proved our conjecture.

Delta: You should call it a *theorem*. There is nothing conjectural about it any more.

Alpha: I wonder. I see that this experiment can be performed for a cube or for a tetrahedron, but how am I to know that it can be performed for *any* polyhedron? For instance, are you sure Sir, that *any polyhedron, after having a face removed, can be stretched flat on the blackboard*? I am dubious about your first step.

Beta: Are you sure that *in triangulating the map one will always get a new face for any new edge*? I am dubious about your second step.

Gamma: Are you sure that *there are only two alternatives – the disappearance of one edge or else of two edges and a vertex – when one drops the triangles one by one*? Are you sure that *one is left with a single triangle at the end of this process*? I am dubious about your third step.

Teacher: Of course I am not sure.

Alpha: But then we are worse off than before! Instead of one conjecture we now have at least three! You call this a 'proof'!

(PR, 7f)

Lakatos requires the mathematician to do two seemingly contradictory things: to prove the conjecture and to refute it. This does not mean to look for a proof, and failing that to seek a counter-example. Rather it means *to give a proof and to give a counter-example as well.* The reason this apparently absurd dictum can actually be carried out is that, according to Lakatos, proofs do not incontrovertibly prove, nor do counter-examples absolutely refute.

When a counter-example to the conjecture is produced (called

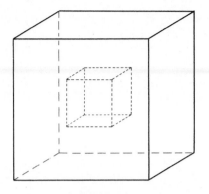

Figure 26

a 'global counter-example'), the proof must be re-examined. We must find, or if need be make up, a lemma which will take the blame for the counter-example. (At this point the counter-example is 'local', since it refutes only the lemma.) The primitive conjecture is then discarded in favour of a new one which contains the lemma in the form of a condition.

> *Alpha*: I have a counter-example which will falsify your first lemma – but this will be a counter-example to the main conjecture, i.e., this will also be a global counter-example as well.
>
> *Teacher*: Indeed! Interesting. Let us see.
>
> *Alpha*: Imagine a solid bounded by a pair of nested cubes – a pair of cubes, one of which is inside, but does not touch the other [Figure 26]. This hollow cube falsifies your first lemma, because removing a face from the inner cube, the polyhedron will not be stretchable on to a plane. Nor will it help to remove a face from the outer cube instead. Besides, for each cube $V - E + F = 2$, so that for the hollow cube $V - E + F = 4$.
>
> *Teacher*: Good show! Let us call it *counter-example 1*. Now what?
>
> *Gamma*: Sir, your composure baffles me. A single counter-example refutes a conjecture as effectively as ten . . .
>
> *Teacher*: I agree with you that the conjecture has received a

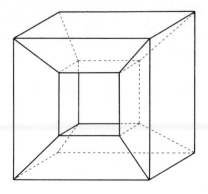

Figure 27

severe criticism by Alpha's counter-example. But it is untrue that the proof has 'completely misfired' . . .

(PR, 13)

After this counter-example and others are proposed and considered, the *picture-frame* becomes the subject of discussion [Figure 27].

> *Teacher*: . . . I for one recognize [the picture-frame] as a genuine global counter-example to the Euler conjecture, as well as a genuine local counter-example to the first lemma of my proof.
>
> *Gamma*: Excuse me, Sir – but how does the picture-frame refute the first lemma?
>
> *Teacher*: First remove a face and then try to stretch it on the blackboard. You will *not* succeed.
>
> *Alpha*: To help your imagination, I will tell you that those and only those polyhedra which you can inflate into a sphere have the property that, after a face is removed, you can stretch the remaining part onto a plane.
>
> It is obvious that such a 'spherical' polyhedron is stretchable onto a plane after a face has been cut out; and vice versa it is equally obvious that, if a polyhedron minus a face is stretchable onto a plane, then you can bend it into a round vase which you can then cover with the missing face, thus getting a spherical polyhedron. But our picture-frame can never be inflated into a sphere; but only into a torus.

Teacher: Good. Now, unlike Delta, I accept this picture-frame as a criticism of the conjecture. I therefore discard the conjecture in its original form as false, but I immediately put forward a modified, restricted version, namely this: the Descartes–Euler conjecture holds good for 'simple' polyhedra, i.e. for those which, after having a face removed, can be stretched onto a plane. Thus we have rescued some of the original hypothesis. . . .

(*PR*, 33f)

And on and on the story goes. This, rather briefly, illustrates *the method of proofs and refutations*.

The key idea in a proof is decomposition. A conjecture is 'proved' by breaking it up into subconjectures. When we see that this is what is really going on in Lakatos, it is not so paradoxical to hear that some conjectures have been both proven and refuted. The Lakatos 'interpretation of proof will allow for a *false* conjecture to be "proved", i.e., to be decomposed into subconjectures. If the conjecture is false, [we] certainly expect at least one of the subconjectures to be false' (*PR*, 23). The key ingredient in the method of proofs and refutations is the method of lemma-incorporation which 'upholds the proof but reduces the domain of the main conjecture to the very domain of the guilty lemma' (*PR*, 34).

Usually philosophers have been concerned with how theories come to be rationally accepted. On the other hand, how theories were thought of initially is a question relegated to psychology. This is Reichenbach's (1938) widely known and accepted distinction between the 'context of discovery' and the 'context of justification'. The latter can be successfully analysed by philosophers, but the former, claims Reichenbach, admits of no rational discussion – there cannot be a rational method of having good ideas. But the method of proofs and refutations flies in the face of this. Not only do proofs justify, but they are the principal device in the generation of new theorems. In this fashion, discovery and justification become intimately connected.

proofs, even though they may not *prove*, certainly do help to *improve* our conjecture. . . . *Our method improves by proving. This intrinsic unity between the 'logic of discovery' and the 'logic of justification' is the most important aspect of the method. . . .*

(PR, 37)

While it is clearly a valuable tool for understanding past mathematics and for creating new, does Lakatos's method have any limitation, in principle? There are cases where application of the Lakatosian heuristic is at least tricky.

Consider the continuum hypothesis (CH) for a moment. This is Cantor's conjecture that $2^{\aleph_0} = \aleph_1$. In contrast with formalists who think it has no truth-value at all, Lakatos would certainly agree that it is either true or false; but which is it? What will the method of proofs and refutations do with this conjecture? Here's one way of seeing the issue: Lakatos's heuristic requires a proof of the conjecture, then a counter-example etc. However, CH is demonstrably independent. That is, by our contemporary standards of what a proof is, and what a counter-example is, CH can neither be proven nor refuted. We may agree with Lakatos that the meta-theory is fallible; perhaps Cohen's independence proof will some day be set aside. Nevertheless, CH is shown to be independent in the *reigning* meta-theory, and that, Lakatos would agree, is the theory we should now use, fallible though it is. (I shall qualify this in a moment.)

The upshot is this: with neither derivation nor counter-example possible, the method of proofs and refutations seems not applicable. It can be of no help in deciding the truth or falsity of CH. Of course, this is not meant to be a knock-down criticism of Lakatos's methods; it is only meant to show a small limitation.

The attitude of many toward CH is that of the hypothetico-deductivist. The conjecture is tested by its consequences. This is the position taken, for example, by Gödel (1947); he rejects CH because it has too many counter-intuitive implications. Lakatos characterizes Gödel as a Euclidean, someone who is methodologically conservative – the greatest of crimes – while the practitioners of the method of proofs and refutations are seen as bold innovators. Ironically, CH may be too bold a conjecture for Lakatos's techniques.

But is this the only way to think of the issue? Perhaps we can come to this question from another side. This is where Lakatos's preference for informal mathematics may prove highly useful.

170

The concept of independence (and hence, the independence of CH) is clearly defined by the first principles involved in settling the issue. These principles are the set of standard axioms and rules of derivation based on standard first-order quantification theory. The whole business is highly formalized. There is neither proof nor refutation of CH in this framework. However, in the informal world of Lakatos, proofs do not start from first principles; they start from the middle and rest on nothing at all. Such an informal proof of CH is indeed possible. It would involve techniques hitherto not contemplated, techniques which we might well be glad to add to our stock methods.

But here I see a happy convergence with attitudes of regular platonists. Though Gödel was inclined to reject CH because of its many counter-intuitive consequences, he thought CH might be settled in the future after we had acquired some new axioms. There is no particular reason to think that we have all the axioms for set theory *now*. After all, Zermelo laid down many of them in 1908; but several years later Fraenkel added more. Future insights may add yet other axioms and these may imply CH (or its negation). So the present independence of CH needn't be fixed for eternity. Un-fixing it could be the future result of an essentially Lakatosian activity.

This type of example illustrates the degree to which formalization can actually play a vital role. It has been essential to a number of great discoveries; the independence of CH, Gödel's incompleteness theorem and even the discovery of non-Euclidean geometry have all rested on the existence of a precise notation and explicit rules of inference. These achievements could never have been made without formalization.

Our mistake, and Lakatos's too, is in confusing preciseness and explicitness with infallibility. We thought we had both. Lakatos shows us we do not have the latter; he tells us we'd be better off without the former. He's half right. We are indeed fallible; but formalization can still be an invaluable tool. Precise notation and explicit rules of inference should be seen in a different light. They are not ends in themselves, nor are they guides to the truth; they are merely devices which are sometimes remarkably useful in the Lakatosian method of proofs and refutations.

THE LATER METHODOLOGY

The editors of his posthumous volume suggest that Lakatos's views on mathematics had changed in the years between its original publication as journal articles in 1962–3 and his death in 1974. They say that had he lived he would have brought *PR* more into line with the views in his remarkable essay 'Falsification and the methodology of scientific research programmes' (hereafter MSRP) published in 1970.

A *research programme*, according to Lakatos, has a *hard core* which is quite immune to revision. This is a set of principles, such as Newton's laws, with which problems are tackled. The hard core plus auxiliary assumptions, known as the *protective belt*, make empirical predictions. A programme is *progressive* if some of its novel predictions are true. When a prediction fails, the protective belt is modified and new predictions are made. Refutations never affect the hard core, only the auxiliary assumptions. To abandon the hard core is to give up the research programme entirely. Rationality, for Lakatos, consists in working on a progressive research programme and abandoning any degenerating one.

Off hand, there seems to be no obvious objection to describing the history of mathematics in terms of the MSRP. (At least there is no objection that has not already been made to its use in accounting for the physical sciences.) If this is so, then it would seem natural for Lakatos to embrace, not attack, the axiomatic method. For example, we may consider the usual axioms of set theory as providing the hard core of the set theory research programme.

For normal scientific theories, progress comes from making successful novel predictions. What would progress be in a mathematical research programme? Michael Hallett (1979) suggests that the aim of any mathematical research programme is the solution of mathematical problems – a programme should decide whether p or $\sim p$ is the case. This seems right, but it can only be part of the answer. One of the great achievements of set theory is its ability to capture within itself all of classical mathematics. Numbers are sets, functions are sets of ordered pairs which are themselves sets etc. The derivation of $2 + 2 = 4$ using only the axioms and concepts of set theory was a great achievement, but hardly the solving of an outstanding mathematical problem. On the other hand, there have been problems which set theory cannot solve – CH for example – but we do not condemn it for that. So it would seem that 'solving problems' is not the complete answer.

Perhaps the situations in mathematics and in the physical sciences are more similar than Hallett thinks. Some mathematical propositions are intuitive. They are a bit like observation statements in the natural sciences. When a set of axioms implies such an intuitive truth, it counts for the truth of the axioms much like the prediction of a novel fact counts for the physical theory which makes the empirical prediction. And if a theory – mathematical or physical – should imply the negation of an intuitive truth or an observable truth, then this should be considered trouble for the theory.

In the light of this, an account of mathematics along the lines of the MSRP seems possible. Of course, this does not detract from Lakatos's central claim: mathematics is fallible. A mathematical research programme may have a hard core which is immune from revision, but the programme itself can be abandoned. Can an MSRP account of mathematics be reconciled with the method of proofs and refutations? We should not be surprised to find some tension. There are certainly differences as well as similarities; but I shall pass over these methodological issues and turn now to matters of ontology.

DEFINITION AND ONTOLOGY

The nature of definition is not much discussed today. Probably because there is a completely dominant view which is apparently unproblematic. It can be found, for example, in *Principia Mathematica*:

> A definition is a declaration that a certain newly-introduced symbol or combination of symbols is to mean the same as a certain other combination of symbols of which the meaning is already known.
>
> It is to be observed that a definition is, strictly speaking, no part of the subject in which it occurs. For a definition is concerned wholly with symbols, not with what they

symbolize. Moreover, it is not true or false, being an expression of a volition, not a proposition.

(Whitehead and Russell 1927, 11)

The same view is sometimes expressed by saying that a definition must satisfy the two criteria of *eliminability* and *noncreativity*; we must always be able to eliminate any defined term in favour of primitive ones, and no new truths should be deducible with the help of definitions that could not be deduced without them. (See, for example, Suppes 1957.) Such a view of definitions is totally foreign to the mathematical world of Lakatos. Let us enter the dialogue at a point where a counter-example has been given to the initial conjecture that $V - E + F = 2$ (which, recall, has already been 'proven').

> *Delta*: But why accept the counter-example? We proved our conjecture – now it is a theorem. I admit that it clashes with this so-called 'counter-example'. One of them has to give way. But why should the theorem give way, when it has been proved? It is the 'criticism' that should retreat. It is fake criticism. This pair of nested cubes is not a counter-example at all. It is a *monster*, a pathological case, not a counter-example.
>
> *Gamma*: Why not? *A polyhedron is a solid whose surface consists of polygonal faces.* And my counter-example is a solid bounded by polygonal faces.
>
> *Teacher*: Let us call this *Def. 1*.
>
> *Delta*: Your definition is incorrect. A polyhedron must be a *surface*: it has faces, edges, vertices, it can be deformed, stretched out on a blackboard, and has nothing to do with the concept of 'solid'. *A polyhedron is a surface consisting of a system of polygons.*
>
> *Teacher*: Call this *Def. 2*.
>
> *Delta*: So really you showed us *two* polyhedra – *two* surfaces, one completely inside the other. A woman with a child in her womb is not a counter-example to the thesis that human beings have one head.
>
> *Alpha*: So! My counter-example has bred a new concept of polyhedron. Or do you dare to assert that by polyhedron you *always* meant surface?
>
> *Teacher*: For the moment let us accept Delta's *Def. 2*. Can

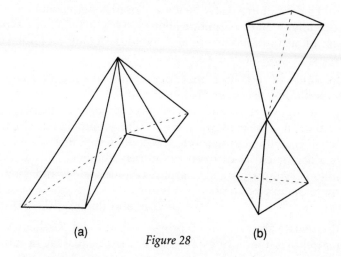

(a)   *Figure 28*   (b)

you refute our conjecture now if by polyhedron we
meant a surface?

Alpha: Certainly. Take two tetrahedra which have an edge
in common [Figure 28(a)]. Or, take two tetrahedra
which have a vertex in common [Figure 28(b)]. Both
these twins are connected, both constitute one single
surface. And, you may check that for both $V - E + F$
$= 3$.

Teacher: *Counter-examples 2a and 2b.*

Delta: I admire your perverted imagination, but of course
I did not mean that *any* system of polygons is a polyhedron. By polyhedron I meant *a system of polygons
arranged in such a way that (1) exactly two polygons meet at
every edge and (2) it is possible to get from the inside of any
polygon to the inside of any other polygon by a route which
never crosses any edge at a vertex.* Your first twins will be
excluded by the first criterion in my definition, your
second twins by the second criterion.

Teacher: *Def. 3.*

(PR, 14f)

Such activity is typical in the history of mathematics and Lakatos
(with qualifications) endorses such definitional jockeying for
position. But in this he is not alone since many proponents of
the standard account of definition might say that not only

should a definition satisfy the above criteria of eliminability and non-creativity, but a definition should also be an adequate explication of an intuitive or pre-analytic idea. Again, according to *Principia Mathematica*:

> In spite of the fact that definitions are theoretically superfluous, it is nevertheless true that they often convey more important information than is contained in the propositions in which they are used. [For example, as] when what is defined is (as often occurs) something already familiar, such as cardinal or ordinal numbers, the definition contains an analysis of a common idea, and may therefore express a notable advance.
>
> (Whitehead and Russell 1927, 11f.)

The debate above over the proper definition of polyhedron is a quarrel over the right explication of the pre-analytic or intuitive idea of a polyhedron. In some respects, this is a worthwhile endeavour, but Lakatos is unhappy. This type of debate often amounts to an essentially conservative intellectual activity – *quelle horreur*. Lakatos has a much more radical account of concept formation.

According to Lakatos, the best way to get better definitions is through proofs. He is something of an essentialist in that he returns to Aristotelian 'real' definitions, definitions which are not merely 'nominal' or stipulative, but are actually true or false. On the other hand, his definitions are not required to capture our pre-analytic, intuitive notions (which makes him somewhat un-Aristotelian). Lakatos's position is quite novel: definitions are theoretical. One reason we keep modifying them is simply that they are fallible attempts to capture our intuitive concepts. But, says Lakatos, there is a second, more important reason: theorizing actually *changes* our concepts. No concept is static; we shall always have to modify our existing definitions (i.e. our linguistic formulations) since conceptual change is an inevitable by-product of theorizing.

> PI: . . . *Proof-generated concepts* are neither 'specifications' nor 'generalizations' of naive concepts. The impact of proofs and refutations on naive concepts is much more revolutionary than that: they *erase* the crucial naive concept completely and replace them by proof-generated concepts.
> . . . In the different proof-generated theorems we have

nothing of the naive concept. That disappeared without a trace. . . . The old problem disappeared, new ones emerged. After Columbus one should not be surprised if *one does not solve the problem one has set out to solve.*

(*PR*, 89f.)

Definitions are conjectures. They are declarative sentences which – if right – assert matters of fact. They are also subject to revision as a result of future theorizing, either because the initial formulation was wrong or because the concept itself has changed in the meantime. Since mathematics does not have a foundation, according to Lakatos, there are no primitive terms (terms explicitly singled out as undefined), and so defined expressions cannot be 'eliminated' (unpacked into a preferred set of primitives). Further, the definitions are obviously 'creative' since we can now derive things with the help of the definition which we could not derive otherwise. Neither of the standard criteria for definitions is satisfied in the Lakatosian way of doing mathematics, which is to say, the way things have often actually been done and the way Lakatos thinks they should be done.

The distinction between definitions and theorems is blurred. Logically, they are on a par – both admit criticism. The difference is methodological – only theorems are proved. Such is the lesson of history, according to Lakatos, and if we want better mathematics, we had better start letting proofs generate our definitions for us, and we should abandon the (formalist inspired) strict insistence on nominal definitions.

Even in a work as revolutionary as *PR*, views are proposed which are similar to those of others. Wittgenstein, for example, shared Lakatos's belief that proofs generate new concepts:

And yet there is something in saying that a mathematical proof creates a new concept. – Every proof is as it were an avowal of a particular employment of signs. . . .

The idea that proof creates a new concept might also be roughly put as follows: a proof is not its foundation plus the rules of inference, but a *new* building – although it is an example of such and such a style. A proof is a *new* paradigm.

(1967, 82)

However, with the generation of concepts by proofs the similarity between Lakatos and Wittgenstein ends, for Wittgenstein is largely a conventionalist while Lakatos is some sort of realist.

As well as with Wittgenstein, there is also a striking similarity with another Cambridge predecessor[3], William Whewell:

> Definitions are rather the last than the first step in each advance. In the progress of real knowledge, these definitions are always the results of the laborious study of individual cases, and are never arrived at by a pure effort of thought, which is what Plato appears to have imagined as the true mode of philosophizing.
>
> (1856, 9)

Like Lakatos, Whewell is an essentialist about definitions – they are not mere stipulations; they are genuinely true or false. Again like Lakatos, Whewell thinks that we don't start with the right concepts at the beginning of an inquiry, but rather that we arrive at them as a *result* of the inquiry. (It is only in this last regard that he differs from Plato.)

Whewell and Lakatos are equally and vehemently opposed to that spirit of inquiry that says define your terms *before* you start; but they differ in one important respect, however. Whewell thinks we can eventually arrive at the correct definition, and know that it is correct. Once we have arrived, infallibility will follow forever after.

> The ideas and definitions which we are thus led to by our inductive process, may bring with them Axioms. Such Axioms may be self-evident as soon as the inductive idea has been distinctly apprehended. . . . And thus Axioms, as well as Definitions may come at the end of our Inductive Propositions; and they thus assume their proper place at the beginning of the deductive propositions which follow them, and are proved from them. . . .
>
> (Whewell 1967, 51)

Though they are separated on this crucial point, Lakatos and Whewell are alike opposed to the usual view of definitions. At least this is so for any *growing* body of knowledge. Perhaps they would both agree, however, with the standard criteria of eliminability and non-creativity for *mature* theories. Whewell would certainly welcome a distinction between growing and mature theories (corresponding to the inductive and deductive stages).

Lakatos, it must be admitted, has an ambivalent attitude toward this matter. At times he distinguishes between the two and qualifies the heuristic method of proofs and refutations as being applicable only to growing theories (*PR*, 42), to what he calls 'informal, quasi-empirical mathematics' (*PR*, 5). But at other times he points out that even mature theories can be rejuvenated. This (rightly) suggests that the distinction between growing and mature theories, if it exists at all, is blurred.

Let us now turn to the related question of ontology, in particular to the question: what is the nature of the realism of *PR*? Though it is clear that *PR* is a realist work of some sort, the issue is not explicitly taken up by Lakatos. Nonetheless, it is difficult to resist speculating.

Platonists fall into distinct camps. They are divided on both epistemological and ontological grounds. All camps maintain that mathematical objects exist independently from us; they are abstract entities, not in space or time. The differences among them first arise when we consider our *access* to the truth. Hardy (1929) and Gödel (1944, 1947) think we can 'see' or somehow or other 'grasp' mathematical objects – not all mathematical truths, perhaps, but at least some. Those truths we cannot directly perceive we guess at, and we test our conjectures by checking their consequences against the intuitive truths.

A weaker brand of Platonism holds that we acquire mathematical knowledge in the same fashion that we acquire physical knowledge – by the ordinary sense perception of physical objects. We know, for example, many things about (abstract) biological species – not by observing them, but by observing (concrete) specimens. Analogously, we know an abundance of mathematics, not because we can directly perceive mathematical objects, but because our mathematical conjectures have had the right consequences for the ordinary physical objects we can see. Quine (1948, 1960) is the foremost champion of this restricted platonism.

Quine's platonism connects mathematical knowledge to ordinary sensory experience, so it could rightly be seen as a kind of mathematical empiricism. And since Lakatos has espoused what he often called 'empiricism' there might be a strong temptation to think of him in the Quinean camp. However, two cautions are in order. First, we should not be misled into thinking Lakatos has *physical* experience (i.e. ordinary sense perception) in mind just because some proof-thought-experiments involve stretching rubber sheets. These 'rubber sheets' have to do things no physical rubber sheet will do. And second, by 'empiricism' Lakatos really means no more than 'fallibilism'; he nowhere implies that mathematical evidence has a physical or sensory nature.

As well as epistemic differences among platonists, there are ontological differences of similar significance. Let's quickly review some of these.

On more than one occasion Popper has expressed approval of Lakatos's philosophy of mathematics. Doubtless, Popper would wish to interpret the realism of *PR* in terms of his 'third world' ontology. Lakatos would likely concur. He has at times made remarks such as this: 'The *products* of knowledge: propositions, theories, systems of theories, problems, problemshifts, research programmes live and grow in the "third world" ' (1978a, 108).

According to Popper, mathematical objects are initially made by us, but take on a life of their own and exist independently of us in the third world. (Worlds one and two contain the physical and the mental, respectively.)

> The third world is not a fiction but exists 'in reality' . . . I suggest *that it is possible to accept the reality or (as it may be called) the autonomy of the third world, and at the same time to admit that the third world originates as a product of human activity.*
>
> (Popper 1972, 159)

And he continues,

> Let us look at the theory of numbers. I believe (unlike Kronecker) that even the natural numbers are the work of men, the product of human language and thought. Yet there is an infinity of such numbers, more than will ever be pronounced by men or used by computers. And there is an infinite number of true equations between such numbers, and of false equations; more than we can ever pronounce as true or false.
>
> But what is even more interesting, unexpected new problems arise as an unintended by-product of the sequence of natural numbers; for instance the unsolved problems of the theory of prime numbers (Goldbach's conjecture, say). These problems are clearly *autonomous*.

They are in no sense made by us; rather they are *discovered* by us; and in this sense they exist, undiscovered, before their discovery.

(Popper 1972, 160)

Kronecker famously remarked that God made the natural numbers; all the rest is the work of humans. But what Kronecker should have said, according to Popper, is that humans made the natural numbers; all the rest is the work of God.

How do we come to know what is and what is not the case in world three?

According to this theory, the human mind can see a physical body in the literal sense of 'see' in which the eyes participate in the process. It can also 'see' or 'grasp' an arithmetical or geometrical object, a number or a geometrical figure. But although in this sense 'see' or 'grasp' is used in a metaphorical way, it nevertheless denotes a real relationship between the mind and its intelligible object, the arithmetical or geometrical object; and the relationship is closely analogous to 'seeing' in the literal sense.

(Popper 1972, 155)

Popper's third world realism, then, is (epistemically) very much akin to the platonism of Gödel and Hardy. The realism of *PR* is perfectly compatible with this, and it is quite possible that Lakatos came to think of mathematical objects as entities in the third world.

If we read *PR* in this world three way (this will be the first of two interpretations), then we can tie Lakatos's realism and his account of definitions together in an interesting way. Mathematical concepts, on this reading, are human creations; the proof-generated technique of defining a polyhedron is a device for creating the best artifact possible. It is a technique for *creating* polyhedra, not for discovering them. (Of course, we cannot be creating polyhedra from scratch. To some extent they are already the 'unintended by-product' of the prior existence of polygons.) The actual revisions in any definition which may occur could stem from either of two sources: the initial characterization of the concept was wrong, or the initial formulation was correct, but in the meantime the concept (which is not identical to its linguistic formulation) has itself undergone a change.

Contrast this with what might be a Lakatosian account of definitions in physics. A scientist defines an 'electron' as a such and such. Lakatos, like any scientific realist, would say that electrons exist independently of the scientist (if they exist at all), and that the definition has a truth-value, it is a fallible conjecture. On the other hand, according to the world three account, polyhedra are not completely independent of the mathematician. Like a table made by a cabinetmaker, they have a life of their own once created; but a dissatisfied cabinetmaker might make another table with different properties – thus changing some truths about tables. And we can discover those properties – that it is three legged, that, in consequence, it doesn't wobble etc. On this account, definitions are true or false, but the fallibilism of any definition of a polyhedron is more like the fallibilism of the truths of the cabinetmaker's tables than it is like the fallibilism of the physicist.

Let me turn now to the more traditional sort of mathematical realism which posits a mathematical realm existing *completely independent* of us, but which we can nevertheless grasp. This will provide a second, and I think superior, interpretation of *PR*.

Mathematical intuition, as I have repeatedly stressed, need not imply certainty. The perception of a platonic realm is quite compatible with Lakatos's fallibilism. In fact, Gödel, himself, thought our perception of sets is slightly out of focus – hence, the paradoxes. In stressing Lakatos's fallibilism we tend to stress the differences between him and traditional platonists like Gödel. This is a mistake; they have much in common. Though *PR* is compatible with Popper's human-made third world, it is equally compatible with traditional platonism. My preference is to read it as embracing the traditional sort rather than Popper's, since Popper's artifact platonism may simply be an untenable account of mathematical ontology. I shall try to provide a (rather fuzzy) argument that this is so.

Consider an outstanding issue in set theory, the conjecture that $V = L$, which says that the universe of sets is exactly the constructible sets. Like CH, it is independent of the rest of set theory. We might again take a hypothetico-deductivist view of $V = L$ when inquiring after its truth, but let us instead consider it in the context of these two different ontological outlooks: traditional platonic realism and Popper's third world realism.

A traditional platonist, on the basis of a 'the more the merrier' principle, will be inclined to think there is much more in the universe of sets than just the constructible ones (there is certainly room for more, logically speaking) and so conclude that $V \neq L$. On the other hand, from the (Popperian) artifact platonist's point of view, the fact that $V = L$ is independent might be considered as evidence for its truth. The reasoning is very simple, though I admit, a bit unorthodox. All there is in world three is what we have explicitly made and all the 'unintended by-products' of our artifacts. We are aware of having made the constructible sets, but not of having made anything else. (This is all the stuff embodied in the standard axioms and no more.) Since $V \neq L$ does not follow from anything we have explicitly or inadvertently done (this is what is meant by independence), it would seem to be the case that the constructible sets are all that we have made, hence, all that exist. Thus, $V = L$ is true.

The situation is not unlike that envisioned by David Lewis (1986) in his concern with the nature of possible worlds. One view says possible worlds are merely consistent sets of sentences. Lewis objects that there are likely to be *ways things could be* that our linguistic resources cannot do justice to; i.e. there are possible worlds which are not linguistically describable. So possible worlds cannot be taken to be sets of sentences; they must instead have an independent reality. Similarly, the traditional mathematical platonist says the tools that are used to build the third world are not powerful enough to do justice to all the sets there could be: some sets are not constructible and some cardinals are inaccessible. From this it follows that sets must have a more independent existence than they would have in Popper's third world.

Lakatos's *PR* can be read either way; polyhedra can be seen as existing in Popper's third world or in Plato's heaven. The method of proofs and refutations is compatible with either. Lakatos's pronouncements, like the one quoted above which explicitly endorses world three, suggest the Popperian reading of *PR*. But there are other remarks of Lakatos worth noting, such as, 'I think that the bulk of logic and mathematics is God's doing and not human convention' (1978b, 127), which I take to be an atheist's way of espousing good old-fashioned platonism.

AFTERWORD

Few contemporary philosophers of science think of themselves as nominalists – but they might as well. Anti-realism and naturalism are certainly the current manifestations of nominalist instincts. Abstract entities and a priori knowledge are looked upon as historical curiosities, as museum pieces like phlogiston and caloric – worthy of our study as historians, perhaps, but unworthy of our belief.

After attacking a small sample of anti-realist and naturalist rivals, I have tried to create a plausible platonism, or at least fill in a few parts of the picture. Is this platonism worthy of our belief? Probably not, at least not yet. Instead, I hope others will view it as I do, as a philosophical research programme. My earlier work on thought experiments, *The Laboratory of the Mind*, is part of that programme, and so is a future book on the philosophy of mathematics. Others are doing related things. Recent work on laws of nature by Tooley and others is particularly exciting; and I take heart in the increasing sympathy (slight though it is) for mathematical platonism and moral realism. But much needs to be done, and (I dare say) to be undone. My hope is that others will take a working interest in these problems. If they do, progress – I am sure – will not be far behind.

NOTES

1 EXPLAINING THE SUCCESS OF SCIENCE

1 I'm going to give an explanation below which is similar to Darwin's in one respect, but it should not be confused with this explanation. Nor should this be confused with the Darwinian epistemology which will be the subject of Chapter 4.

2 The idea is that laws and theories generally are false, but the things they talk about (at least the ones with causal capacities, e.g. electrons, genes, etc.) are quite real and certainly exist, according to Cartwright.

3 See his 'Statistical explanation' (1971). More recent is his *Scientific Explanation and the Causal Structure of the World* (1984).

4 There are problems with this account; see, for example, the relevant discussion by Cartwright in *How the Laws of Physics Lie* (1983). Salmon has further fine tuned his view in *Scientific Explanation and the Causal Structure of the World* (1984).

5 For example, Goudge (1961) and Dray (1964).

3 LATOUR'S PROSAIC SCIENCE

1 A new edition (a reprint by Princeton University Press) drops the word 'Social' from the title on the grounds that it is so obvious as not to need mentioning.

2 For example, Harry Collins in his *Changing Order* (1985) takes the same general outlook to science: existence of facts and acceptance of instruments go hand in hand.

3 Brian Baigrie has rightly stressed (private communication) that the network contains much more than propositions. I entirely agree. See his forthcoming collection, *Scientific Illustrations*, to see one important type of non-propositional element in science. It remains in the case at hand, however, that propositional or not Latour's envisaged network is very small.

4 For a critical discussion of how social factors can influence the

content of science in a variety of ways see my earlier book, *The Rational and the Social* (1989).

5 The relation between belief dissemination in scientific society and in general society is an interesting one. Baigrie (private communication) remarks:

> Latour conflates two distinct scenarios: the process whereby beliefs are certified in the scientific community and the process whereby beliefs are disseminated throughout the population at large. The question is how and why expert beliefs are accepted by non-experts; but Latour collapses the first question into the second and asks: why do beliefs that are widely accepted seem to arise from a special community of experts? He takes the second question to be fundamental and so holds that what is true for a community as a whole is true of specialized groups. There is no diversity, on this view, and no real expertise. Just the dissemination of knowledge.

6 Bloor's symmetry principle calls for the same type of explanation for any belief regardless of its truth or falsity, its rationality or irrationality etc. See Bloor, *Knowledge and Social Imagery* (1976/1991, 5), and Brown, *The Rational and Social* (1989, ch. 2), for a critique.

7 The *locus classicus* on the topic is Donald Davidson's 'Actions, reasons, and causes' reprinted in Davidson (1980). A brief discussion of this issue in connection with the strong programme can be found in Brown (1989, 24ff.).

4 THE NATURALISM OF RUSE

1 An excellent recent critique is B. Baigrie, 'Natural selection vs trial and error elimination' (1988).

2 It is actually hard to say whether the Reagans have suffered more by being associated with astrology, or astrology by having the Reagans take it seriously. It would be nice to see them go down the drain together, but we should not be sanguine about the prospects of this happening.

3 For detailed criticisms see Brown, 'Rescher's evolutionary epistemology' (1985).

4 Hume (*Treatise*, 483f.). Hume's naturalism is every bit as important as his scepticism; indeed, they are linked. See, for example, Stroud, *Hume* (1977).

5 Some discussion of these issues can be found in Brown, 'Rescher's evolutionary epistemology' (1985).

6 See Kuhn, *The Structure of Scientific Revolutions* (1962/1970), and Churchland, *Scientific Realism and the Plasticity of Mind* (1979), for examples of this outlook.

7 Boyd, 'Scientific realism and naturalistic epistemology' (1981); Laudan, *Science and Values* (1984).

8 This is the same sort of objection some evolutionary biologists, e.g. S. J. Gould and R. Lewontin, raise against sociobiology.

9 For example in 'Philosophy and the scientific image of man' (1962).

5 PUTNAM'S VERIFICATION

1 Putnam's realist period work is collected in the first two volumes of his *Philosophical Papers* (1975a & b). The anti-realist period started with *Meaning and the Moral Sciences* (1976) and hit full stride in *Reason, Truth, and History* (1981). The third volume of his *Philosophical Papers* (1983) and the more recent collection of essays *Realism with a Human Face* (1990) continue in the same anti-realist vein.

6 KNOWLEDGE – IN THE ABSTRACT

1 Following this one Hume gave two other definitions which he seemed to think were equivalent. They aren't, but they are in the same regularity spirit: 'if the first object had not been, the second never had existed'. And 'an object followed by another, and whose appearance always conveys the thought to that other'.
2 Representative samples can be found in the volume edited by Hilary Kornblith, *Naturalizing Epistemology* (1985).
3 See, for example, P. Benacerraf, 'Mathematical truth' (1973), and H. Field, *Science Without Numbers* (1980).
4 For a thorough account of early interpretations of QM (as well as present-day ones) see M. Jammer, *The Philosophy of Quantum Mechanics* (1974).
5 Aspect *et al.* 'Experimental tests of realistic theories via Bell's theorem' (1981), 'Experimental realization of Einstein–Podolsky–Rosen *Gedankenexperiment*: a new violation of Bell's inequalities' (1982a), 'Experimental test of Bell's inequalities using time-varying analyzers' (1982b).
6 For a spectrum of views on this issue see Pappas and Swain (eds), *Knowledge and Justified Belief* (1978).
7 Otherwise I could perform the thought experiment now and derive 'The moon is made of green cheese'.
8 For example by Fischbach *et al.* 'Reanalysis of the Eötvos experiment' (1986). I suspect that the reason that Galileo's thought experiment works for light/heavy but not for colours is that the former are adjective or extensive while the later are not (i.e. combining two red objects will not make an object twice as red).

7 PHENOMENA

1 This term is unfortunately loaded. Sociologists of science often use 'construction' to mean 'social construction', the very opposite of an independently existing 'fact'. I am using the term in a more innocuous sense perfectly compatible with describing the objective truth. For example, when a mathematician 'constructs' a function, he or she is not creating it anew, but merely (though perhaps very cleverly) characterizing it in terms of other already given mathematical objects.
2 This challenge came from Simon Blackburn during a conference when a version of this material was presented.

3 For more on natural kind reasoning see Harper (1989). Generally, this is unexplored territory; it deserves a great deal more attention.
4 Thanks to Mary Tiles for making this point; I am grateful to her for helpful discussions on a number of other topics in this book as well.
5 See the interesting and important article by G. Hon (1989).

8 WHAT IS THE VECTOR POTENTIAL?

1 A brief conversation with Jed Buchwald made me realize some of the historical complexities involved in the following line of reasoning, in particular concerning the subtleties involved in the localization of energy.
2 Maxwell's opinion is not entirely clear. Margaret Morrison (to whom I am grateful for the information) thinks that Maxwell was probably agnostic about the physical versus mathematical status of the vector potential.
3 The first of these was by Chambers (1960); more recent experimental results are reported in Tonomura (1986), Tonomura *et al.* (1986) and van Loosdrecht *et al.* (1988).
4 See J. Wheeler, 'Law without law', in Wheeler and Zurek (eds) (1983), for a discussion of delayed-choice experiments in quantum mechanics.

9 PROOF AND TRUTH IN THE ABSTRACT REALM

1 Though it was published posthumously; two other volumes of collected papers, Lakatos (1978a, b), were published after his death in 1974.
2 This doctrine is only in embryonic form in *PR*; its full development is to be found in the essay written later, 'Falsification and the methodology of scientific research programmes' (1970).
3 Lakatos wrote the first version of *PR* while a graduate student at Cambridge. The work is avowedly Popperian; however, there are less obvious, but no less strong, Cambridge influences.

BIBLIOGRAPHY

Aharonov, Y. and D. Bohm (1959) 'Significance of electromagnetic potentials in the quantum theory', *Physical Review*.

Armstrong, D. (1983) *What is a Law of Nature?*, Cambridge: Cambridge University Press.

Aspect, A. *et al.* (1981) 'Experimental tests of realistic theories via Bell's theorem', *Physical Review Letters* 47, (7), 460–3.

Aspect, A. *et al.* (1982a) 'Experimental realization of Einstein–Podolsky–Rosen *Gedankenexperiment*: a new violation of Bell's inequalities', *Physical Review Letters*, 49, (2).

Aspect, A. *et al.* (1982b) 'Experimental test of Bell's inequalities using time-varying analyzers', *Physical Review Letters* 49, (25).

Ayer, A. J. (1956) 'What is a law of nature?', reprinted in T. Beauchamp (ed.) *Philosophical Problems of Causation*, Encino, CA: Dickenson, 1974.

Baigrie, B. (1988) 'Natural selection vs trial and error elimination', *International Studies in the Philosophy of Science*.

Ballentine, L. (1990) *Quantum Mechanics*, Englewood Cliffs, NJ: Prentice-Hall.

Barnes, B. (1985) *About Science*, Oxford: Blackwell.

Benacerraf, P. (1973) 'Mathematical truth', reprinted in P. Benacerraf and H. Putnam (eds) *The Philosophy of Mathematics*, 2nd edn, Cambridge: Cambridge University Press, 1983.

Bloor, D. (1976/1991) *Knowledge and Social Imagery*, 2nd edn, Chicago, IL: University of Chicago Press.

Bogen, J. and J. Woodward (1988) 'To save the phenomena', *Philosophical Review*.

Bohr, N. (1934) *Atomic Theory and the Description of Nature*, Cambridge: Cambridge University Press.

Bohr, N. (1958) *Atomic Physics and Human Knowledge*, New York: Wiley.

Bohr, N. (1963) *Essays 1959–1962 on Atomic Physics and Human Knowledge*, New York: Wiley.

Boyd, R. (1981) 'Scientific realism and naturalistic epistemology', in P. Asquith and R. Giere (eds) *PSA 1980*, vol. II.

Braithwaite, R. B. (1953) *Scientific Explanation*, Cambridge: Cambridge University Press.

Brown, J. R. (1985) 'Rescher's evolutionary epistemology', *Philosophia*.
Brown, J. R. (1989) *The Rational and the Social*, London: Routledge.
Brown, J. R. (1990) 'π in the Sky', in A. Irvine (ed.) *Physicalism in Mathematics*, Dordrecht: Kluwer.
Brown, J. R. (1991) *The Laboratory of the Mind: Thought Experiments in the Natural Sciences*, London: Routledge.
Cartwright, N. (1983) *How the Laws of Physics Lie*, Oxford: Oxford University Press.
Cartwright, N. (1989) *Nature's Capacities and their Measurement*, Oxford: Oxford University Press.
Chambers, R. G. (1960) *Physical Review Letters*.
Churchland, P. (1979) *Scientific Realism and the Plasticity of Mind*, Cambridge: Cambridge University Press.
Collins, H. (1985) *Changing Order: Replication and Induction in Scientific Practice*, London: Sage.
Davidson, D. (1963) 'Actions, reasons, and causes', reprinted in D. Davidson *Essays on Actions and Events*, Oxford: Oxford University Press, 1980.
Davidson, D. (1980) *Essays on Actions and Events*, Oxford: Oxford University Press.
Dray, W. (1964) *Philosophy of History*, Englewood Cliffs, NJ: Prentice-Hall.
Dretske, F. (1977) 'Laws of nature', *Philosophy of Science*.
Dummett, M. (1963) 'Realism', reprinted in *Truth and Other Enigmas*, Cambridge, MA: Harvard University Press, 1978.
Earman, J. (1986) *A Primer on Determinism*, Dordrecht: Reidel.
Einstein, A. (1921) 'Geometry and experience', reprinted in *Ideas and Opinions*, New York: Bonanza Books, 1954.
Einstein, A. and L. Infeld (1938) *The Evolution of Physics*, New York: Simon and Schuster.
Einstein, A., Podolsky and Rosen (1935) 'Can quantum mechanical description of reality be considered complete?', *Physical Review*.
Feynman, R. (1963) *The Feynman Lectures in Physics*, 3 vols., Reading, MA: Addison-Wesley.
Feynman, R. (1985) *QED: The Strange Story of Light and Matter*, Princeton, NJ: Princeton University Press.
Field, H. (1980) *Science Without Numbers*, Oxford: Blackwell.
Fine, A. (1986) *The Shaky Game*, Chicago, IL: Chicago University Press.
Fischbach et al. (1986) 'Reanalysis of the Eötvos experiment', *Physical Review Letters* (Jan.).
Frank, J. and G. Hertz (1914a) 'Über Zusammenstösse zwischen Electronen und den Molekülen des Quecksilberdampfes und die Ionisierungsspannung desselben', *Verhandlungen der Deutschen Physikalischen Gesellschaft, Berlin* 16, 457.
Frank, J. and G. Hertz (1914b) 'Über die erregung der Quecksilberresonanzlinie 253.6 $\mu\mu$ durch Elektronenstösse', *Verhandlungen der Deutschen Physikalischen Gesellschaft, Berlin* 16, 512.
van Fraassen, B. (1980) *The Scientific Image*, Oxford: Oxford University Press.

van Fraassen, B. (1989) *Laws and Symmetry*, Oxford: Oxford University Press.

Galileo (*Dialogo*) *Dialogues on the Two Chief World Systems*, trans. S. Drake, Berkeley, CA: University of California Press, 1953.

Galileo (*Discoursi*) *Discourse on Two New Sciences*, trans. S. Drake, Madison, WI: University of Wisconsin Press, 1974.

Gödel, K. (1944) 'Russell's mathematical logic', reprinted in P. Benacerraf and H. Putnam, (eds) *Philosophy of Mathematics*, Cambridge: Cambridge University Press, 1983.

Gödel, K. (1947) 'What is Cantor's continuum problem?', reprinted in P. Benacerraf and H. Putnam, (eds) *Philosophy of Mathematics*, Cambridge: Cambridge University Press, 1983.

Goodman, N. (1947) 'The problem of counter-factual conditionals', reprinted in *Fact, Fiction, and Forcast*, Indianapolis, IN: Hackett, 1973.

Goudge, T. (1961) *The Ascent of Life*, London: George Allen & Unwin.

Hacking, I. (1983) *Representing and Intervening*, Cambridge: Cambridge University Press.

Hacking, I. (1988) 'The participant irrealist at large in the laboratory', *British Journal for the Philosophy of Science*.

Hacking, I. (forthcoming) 'The disunities of science'.

Hallett, M. (1979) 'Towards a theory of mathematical research programmes I and II', *British Journal for the Philosophy of Science*.

Harding, S. (1986) *The Science Question in Feminism*, Ithaca, NY: Cornell University Press.

Harding, S. (1991) *Whose Science? Whose Knowledge?*, Ithaca, NY: Cornell University Press.

Hardy, G.H. (1929) 'Mathematical proof', *Mind*.

Harper, W. (1989) 'Conscilience and natural kind reasoning', in J. Brown and J. Mittelstrass (eds) *An Intimate Relation: Studies in the History and Philosophy of Science*, Dordrecht: Kluwer.

Harper, W. (1990) 'Newtons classical deductions from phenomena', in A. Fine, M. Forbes and L. Wessels (eds) *PSA 1990*.

Heisenberg, W. (1958) *Physics and Philosophy*, New York: Harper and Row.

Hempel, C. (1965) *Aspects of Scientific Explanation*, New York: Free Press.

Hon, G. (1989) 'Frank and Hertz versus Townsend: a study of two types of experimental error', *Historical Studies in the Physical Sciences* 20 (1).

Hume, D. (*Treatise*) *Treatise on Human Nature*, Oxford: Oxford University Press, 1888.

Hume, D. (*Enquiry*) *Enquiry Concerning Human Understanding*, Oxford: Oxford University Press, 1975.

Jammer, M. (1974) *The Philosophy of Quantum Mechanics*, New York: Wiley.

Joule, J. (1850) 'On the mechanical equivalent of heat', *Philosophical Transactions of the Royal Society*.

Kahneman, D. et al. (eds) (1982) *Judgment Under Uncertainty: Heuristics and Biases*, Cambridge: Cambridge University Press.

Kaiser, M. (1991) 'From rocks to graphs – the shaping of phenomena', *Synthèse*, 111–33.

191

Kaiser, M. (forthcoming) 'Empirical versus theoretical progress in science'.

van Kampen, N. G. (1984) 'Can the Aharonov–Bohm effect transmit signals faster than light?', *Physics Letters* 106A (1), 2.

Kornblith, H. (1985) *Naturalizing Epistemology*, Cambridge, MA: MIT Press.

Kripke, S. (1972) *Naming and Necessity* (originally published as an article, reprinted as a book) Oxford: Blackwell, 1980.

Kuhn, T. S. (1962/1970) *The Structure of Scientific Revolutions*, 2nd edn, Chicago, IL: University of Chicago Press.

Lakatos, I. (1970) 'Falsification and the methodology of scientific research programmes', reprinted in I. Lakatos *The Methodology of Scientific Research Programmes: Philosophical Papers*, vol. I, Cambridge: Cambridge University Press.

Lakatos, I. (1976) *Proofs and Refutations: The Logic of Mathematical Discovery*, Cambridge: Cambridge University Press.

Lakatos, I. (1978a) *The Methodology of Scientific Research Programmes: Philosophical Papers*, vol. I, Cambridge: Cambridge University Press.

Lakatos, I. (1978b) *Mathematics, Science, and Epistemology: Philosophical Papers*, vol. II, Cambridge: Cambridge University Press.

Landau, L. and E. M. Lifshitz (1975) *The Classical Theory of Fields*, London: Pergamon.

Latour, B. and S. Woolgar (1979) *Laboratory Life: The Social Construction of Scientific Facts*, London: Sage.

Latour, B. (1987) *Science in Action: How to Follow Scientists and Engineers Through Society*, Cambridge, MA: Harvard University Press.

Latour, B. (1988) *The Pasteurization of France*, (trans. A. Sheridan and J. Law from *Les Microbes: Guerre et Paix suivi de Irréductions*, Paris, 1984), Cambridge, MA: Harvard University Press.

Laudan, L. (1977) 'Sources of modern methodology', reprinted in L. Laudan *Science and Hypothesis*, Dordrecht: Reidel, 1981.

Laudan, L. (1981) 'A confutation of convergent realism', *Philosophy of Science*.

Laudan, L. (1984) *Science and Values*, Berkeley, CA: University of California Press.

Leplin. J. (1980) 'The historical objection to scientific realism', in P. Asquith and R. Giere (eds) *PSA 1980*, vol. I.

Lewis, D. (1973) *Counterfactuals*, Oxford: Blackwell.

Lewis, D. (1986) *On the Plurality of Worlds*, Oxford: Blackwell.

Longino, H. (1989) *Science as Social Knowledge: Values and Objectivity in Scientific Inquiry*, Princeton, NJ: Princeton University Press.

van Loosdrecht, P. H. M., *et al.* (1988) 'Aharonov–Bohm effect in a singly connected point contact', *Physical Review B*, (Nov.).

Lorentz, H. A. (1915) *Theory of Electrons*, reprinted by Dover, New York, 1952.

Lorenz, K. (1941) 'Kant's doctrine of the a priori in the light of contemporary biology', reprinted in H. Plotkin (ed.) *Learning, Development, and Culture: Essays in Evolutionary Epistemology*, New York: Wiley, 1982.

Maxwell, J. C. (1871) *Theory of Heat*, London: Longman.
Maxwell, J. C. (1890) *Scientific Papers of J. C. Maxwell*, Cambridge: Cambridge University Press.
Maxwell, J. C. (1891) *A Treatise on Electricity and Magnetism*, Oxford: Clarendon.
Nagel, E. (1961) *The Structure of Science*, New York: Harcourt, Brace and World.
Neurath, O. (1955) 'Unified science as encyclopedic integration', in O. Neurath, R. Carnap and W. Morris (eds) *International Encyclopedia of Unified Science*, Chicago, IL: University of Chicago Press.
Newton-Smith, W. H. (1981) *The Rationality of Science*, London: Routledge & Kegan Paul.
Pappas, G. and M. Swain (eds) (1978) *Knowledge and Justified Belief*, Ithaca, NY: Cornell University Press.
Papineau, D. (1987) *Reality and Representation*, Oxford: Blackwell.
Penrose, R. (1989) *The Emperor's New Mind*, Oxford: Oxford University Press.
Popper, K. (1972) *Objective Knowledge*, Oxford: Oxford University Press.
Putnam, H. (1975a) *Philosophical Papers*, vol. I, Cambridge: Cambridge University Press.
Putnam, H. (1975b) *Philosophical Papers*, vol II, Cambridge: Cambridge University Press.
Putnam, H. (1975c) 'The meaning of meaning', reprinted in H. Putnam *Philosophical Papers*, vol. II, Cambridge: Cambridge University Press.
Putnam, H. (1976) *Meaning and the Moral Sciences*, London: Routledge & Kegan Paul.
Putnam, H. (1981) *Reason, Truth, and History*, Cambridge: Cambridge University Press.
Putnam, H. (1983) *Philosophical Papers*, vol. III, Cambridge: Cambridge University Press.
Putnam, H. (1984) 'The craving for objectivity', reprinted in H. Putnam *Realism with a Human Face*, Cambridge, MA: Harvard University Press.
Putnam, H. (1990) *Realism with a Human Face*, Cambridge, MA: Harvard University Press.
Putnam, H. and P. Oppenheim (1958) 'Unity of science as a working hypothesis', in Feigl, Scriven and Maxwell (eds) *Concepts, Theories, and the Mind–Body Problem, Minnesota Studies in the Philosophy of Science*, Minneapolis, MN: University of Minnesota Press.
Quine, W. V. (1948) 'On what there is', reprinted in *From a Logical Point of View*, Cambridge, MA: Harvard University Press, 1953.
Quine, W. V. (1960) *Word and Object*, Cambridge, MA: Harvard University Press.
Quine, W. V. (1969) 'Epistemology naturalized', in *Ontological Relativity and Other Essays*, New York: Columbia University Press.
Ramsey, F. (1931) *Foundations of Mathematics*, London: Routledge & Kegan Paul.
Reichenbach, H. (1938) *Experience and Prediction*, Chicago, IL: Chicago University Press.

Rescher, N. (1977) *Methodological Pragmatism*, Oxford: Blackwell.
Rorty, R. (1979) *Philosophy and the Mirror of Nature*, Princeton, NJ: Princeton University Press.
Rorty, R. (1985) 'Solidarity or objectivity?', reprinted in R. Rorty *Objectivity, Relativism, and Truth*, Cambridge: Cambridge University Press, 1991.
Rorty, R. (1987) 'Science as solidarity', reprinted in R. Rorty *Objectivity, Relativism, and Truth*, Cambridge: Cambridge University Press, 1991.
Rorty, R. (1988a) 'Is natural science a natural kind?', reprinted in R. Rorty *Objectivity, Relativism, and Truth*, Cambridge: Cambridge University Press, 1991.
Rorty, R. (1988b) 'The priority of democracy to philosophy', reprinted in R. Rorty *Objectivity, Relativism, and Truth*, Cambridge: Cambridge University Press, 1991.
Rorty, R. (1989) *Contingency, Irony, and Solidarity*, Cambridge: Cambridge University Press.
Rorty, R. (1991) *Objectivity, Relativism, and Truth*, Cambridge: Cambridge University Press.
Ruse, M. (1986) *Taking Darwin Seriously: A Naturalistic Approach to Philosophy*, Oxford: Blackwell.
Salmon, W. (1971) 'Statistical explanation', reprinted in W. Salmon (ed.) *Statistical Explanation and Statistical Relevance*, Pittsburgh, PA: Pittsburgh University Press, 1971.
Salmon, W. (1984) *Scientific Explanation and the Causal Structure of the World*, Princeton, NJ: Princeton University Press.
Schiebinger, L. (1989) *The Mind Has No Sex?*, Cambridge, MA: Harvard University Press.
Schweber, S. (1985) 'Feynman and the visualization of space–time processes', *Review of Modern Physics* 58 (2).
Sellars, W. (1961) 'The language of theories', reprinted in *Science, Perception, and Reality*, London: Routledge & Kegan Paul, 1963.
Sellars, W. (1962) 'Philosophy and the scientific image of man', reprinted in *Science, Perception, and Reality*, London: Routledge & Kegan Paul, 1963.
Smart, J. J. C. (1968) *Between Science and Philosophy*, New York: Random House.
Stroud, B. (1977) *Hume*, London: Routledge & Kegan Paul.
Suppes, P. (1957) *Introduction to Logic*, New York: Van Nostrand.
Tonomura, A. (1986) 'Experimental confirmation of the Aharonov–Bohm effect by electron holography', in L. Roth and A. Inomata (eds) *Fundamental Questions in Quantum Mechanics*, New York: Gordon and Breach.
Tonomura, A. et al. (1986) 'Evidence for Aharonov–Bohm effect with magnetic field completely shielded from electron wave', *Physical Review Letters* 58 (8).
Tooley, M. (1977) 'The nature of laws', *Canadian Journal of Philosophy*.
Tooley, M. (1988) *Causation: A Realist Approach*, Oxford: Oxford University Press.

Toulmin, S. (1972) *Human Understanding*, Princeton, NJ: Princeton University Press.

Trigg, G. (1975) *Landmark Experiments in 20th Century Physics*, New York: Crane, Russell.

Wheeler, J. and W. Zurek (eds) (1983) *Quantum Theory and Measurement*, Princeton, NJ: Princeton University Press.

Whewell, W. (1856) *On the Philosophy of Discovery* (modern reprint), New York: Franklin.

Whewell, W. (1858) *Novum Organon Renovatum*, 3rd edn, London.

Whewell, W. (1967) *William Whewell's Theory of Scientific Method*, ed. R. E. Butts, Pittsburgh, PA: University of Pittsburgh Press.

Whitehead, A. N. and B. Russell (1927) *Principia Mathematica*, 2nd edn, Cambridge: Cambridge University Press.

Wigner, E. (1962) 'Remarks on the mind–body problem', reprinted in *Symmetries and Reflections*, Cambridge, MA: MIT Press, 1967.

Wigner, E. (1964) 'Two kinds of reality', reprinted in *Symmetries and Reflections*, Cambridge, MA: MIT Press, 1967.

Wilson, E. O. (1975) *Sociobiology: The New Synthesis*, Cambridge, MA: Harvard University Press.

Wittgenstein, L. (1967) *Remarks on the Foundations of Mathematics*, 2nd edn, Oxford: Blackwell.

Woodward, J. (1989) 'Data and phenomena', *Synthèse*.

INDEX